Military

RECORDS

AT ANCESTRY.COM

★　★　★

ESTHER YU SUMNER

 ancestry publishing

Copyright © 2007
The Generations Network, Inc.

Published by
Ancestry Publishing, a division of The Generations Network, Inc.
360 West 4800 North
Provo, Utah 84604
www.ancestry.com

Library of Congress Cataloging-in-Publication Data

Sumner, Esther Yu.
    Military records at Ancestry.com / Esther Yu Sumner.
        p. cm.
    Includes bibliographical references and index.
    ISBN 978-1-59331-311-1 (alk. paper)
1. United States—Genealogy—Computer network resources—Handbooks, manuals, etc. 2. Soldiers—United States—Genealogy—Computer network resources—Handbooks, manuals, etc. 3. Ancestry.com (Firm) 4. United States—History, Military—Bibliography. 5. United States—History, Military—Computer network resources. 6. United States—History, Military—Miscellanea. I. Title.

    CS49.S86 2007
    929'.10285—dc22

2007021919

10 9 8 7 6 5 4 3 2 1

ISBN-13: 978-1-59331-311-1
ISBN-10: 1-59331-311-X

Created in the United States of America

★ ★ ★

TABLE OF CONTENTS

LIST OF ILLUSTRATIONS

Many of the images in this book are available for purchase from Ancestry.com at The Ancestry Store <www.theancestrystore.com>. Below you will find the title and description of each image, as well as the page in this book on which it is located.

INTRODUCTION

THE BUGLER STOOD ALONE in the shade of an oak tree, positioned so far away from the flag-covered casket that his presence went largely unnoticed. Against the bright sky, he was nothing more than a silhouette in uniform.

He lifted his bugle to his lips and sent the solemn notes of "Taps" up through the air. The contrast of the somber tune against the calm July air was odd, yet fitting. The family of Robert Alder Sumner was at peace with his passing, but they grieved that he would no longer be just a phone call or short visit away. The World War II U.S. Air Force pilot, a much-loved and much-respected man, had left the world.

Robert Sumner did not talk a great deal about the war, but in the last weeks of his life, its influence became more and more apparent. He began recalling memories from the war. At his viewing and funeral, the displays depicting moments of his life included the uniform he'd worn and a sketch of the airplane he had flown.

During the funeral, his eldest son shared a letter that Robert had written to his wife while in the service, rejoicing at the news that his first child had been born. His affection for his wife and for the son he had not yet met was very apparent. This son would later follow in his footsteps, serving the United States in the army. Also, in the following generation, another son would carry on the tradition, the husband of Robert's granddaughter.

Despite their close relationship with their father, Robert's children still have questions that he can no longer answer. What stories did he leave the world without telling his descendants? The family was amazed by the amount of records about Robert's past and about the war that nobody knew were tucked away into the attic until the family began cleaning out the house.

At least one member of the Sumner family has served in the military in each of the last three generations. How many generations back does the Sumner family carry on that tradition of serving their nation? What were their real stories and experiences? It is a special experience to hear these stories firsthand, but even when your military ancestors are no longer available to share them, many are still waiting to be discovered.

We can fill in the details we do not know, things that our ancestors may not have wanted to remember or discuss, by looking for clues in military records. When did they serve? Did they receive a pension for their service? What was their rank? The stories are waiting to be discovered in U.S. military records.

The importance of military records

THERE HAVE BEEN SO MANY MILITARY CONFLICTS in American history that any of our ancestors who lived in the United States almost certainly lived through one.

From 1622, when the colonists' conflicts with the Indians escalated into war, to involvement with Iraq in the twenty-first century, the United States has been involved in over forty wars or conflicts, many lasting less than a year, some spanning close to a decade. In some wars, we have been fortunate enough to not lose any lives. In the Civil War, Americans lost an estimated 525,000 lives, though higher numbers have been recorded. In World War I, we lost more than 115,000 American lives, though the worldwide total was more than 9 million people. In World War II, Americans lost more than 290,000 lives during battle and more than 113,000 lives to other causes. The overall deaths in the combined countries were between 40 and 50 million lives.

Even if a specific ancestor did not serve in America's armed forces during a war through which they lived, they likely had a sibling, cousin, or more distant relative who served in the war. Some of us are lucky enough to have parents and grandparents pass down their military stories to us verbally, but even without oral stories, or in addition to these oral stories, we can piece together more about our ancestors by researching in military records.

War brought about change

We rely on these military records to fill in the gaps because military stories are often among the most exciting tales shared about our ancestors. They tell us about acts of bravery, moments of tragedy and sorrow, and tales of heroism, and they give us background on how our ancestors' lives were shaped. War sent soldiers to new soil for battle, sometimes bringing home foreign brides. War brought about change, shifting boundaries between and within countries and affecting the governments under which people were ruled. War resulted in millions of deaths as a result of battle, disease, and even poverty, affecting both the general economy and personal status of individuals who became widows or who lost parents or children, saw their property and home destroyed, or, in some cases, were awarded land. War resulted in the migration of individuals, some seeking to rebuild in a new location.

Military records tell a story

Military records are an exciting place to do genealogy research because if we know the war in which an ancestor fought, we can already begin gathering a story about that ancestor by learning about the war. Along with U.S. census records, birth and death records, and marriage records, military records are among the most reliable sources for finding a record about an individual. This is because of the scope of war and the likelihood of each individual with American ancestors to have seen military service in his or her family.

Researching in military records is rewarding because the chances of success are good. A researcher needs to be pointed in the right direction, rather than just walking blindly into a library and assuming a librarian can magically provide the desired records. However, with a little bit of preliminary research, like finding out possible variations of an ancestor's name, the general lifespan of the individual, and the potential wars in which the ancestor was involved, a researcher can find success.

Take a look at the draft registration cards of famous men on the next page to see what stories they tell us.

Understanding military records—the basics

FOR THE MAJORITY OF THE WARS in which Americans were involved, records were made and kept at a combination of federal, state, and local levels. While military records are an exciting source of information about our ancestors, they were not kept with genealogy research in mind, but for government purposes. Therefore, many of these records are available in different locations in the United States, which might mean an airplane trip or a cross-country drive. Some of the best resources are the records available at the National Archives, located in Washington, D.C., or at state archives and historical societies.

However, with the World Wide Web, and by ordering records through the mail, researchers can find a lot of initial information without having to travel far. The National Archives does offer some of their records online, though the majority of their records are in-house. The Generations Network, the parent company of Ancestry Publishing, offers more than 175 military collections online, a total of over 90 million names, with more on the way.

What types of records were created because of war?

Some military records are gold mines of information about individuals, some are more uneven in the information they offer, and some give very little detail but may still be useful as clues to further information.

Examples of some of the records from which you can learn include the following:

- Draft registration cards—Originally developed during the Civil War, draft registration meant to

The **World War I draft registration card** for famous poet e e cummings (Edward E. Cummings) tells us that he was born on 14 October 1894 and was twenty-three when he completed the draft form. The field for the registrar's description of Cummings height was initially "tall," but this is crossed out and replaced with "medium." We also learn that, at that time, Cummings indicated his occupation as "student." The draft registration card also tells us that Cummings served in the Norton-Harjes (Ambulance Corp) in France. From other sources, we learn that he actually spent three and a half months in a concentration camp while there. For the item in which Cummings could indicate if he was in any way disabled, a somewhat difficult to decipher sentence indicates something to the effect of being "home on account of illness." Cummings was drafted into the army during the last year of World War I.

Like Cummings, the famous **artist Norman Rockwell** was also twenty-three when he completed his draft registration card in June 1917. We learn from his draft registration that he was born on 3 February 1894 and that already at that age he declared his occupation to be an "artist," working as a "freelancer." We also learn that unlike Cummings, he was married when he registered for the draft and had no previous military experience. The registrar report for Rockwell indicated that he was tall, with brown hair and brown eyes.

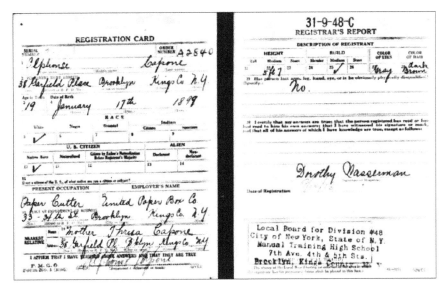

Famous gangster Alphonse "Al" Capone completed a different version of the draft registration card than Cummings and Rockwell. His card, Registration Card C, tells us that when he registered in September 1918, he was nineteen years old and was working as a paper cutter for the United Paper Box Co. At that time, he lived in Brooklyn, and at five feet seven inches, had a slender build, gray eyes, and dark brown hair.

ensure that armies had enough soldiers to fight in their wars. Each draft record contains information about individuals who registered for a military draft. In 1917 and 1918, close to 25 percent of the U.S. population registered for the World War I draft. That 25 percent encompasses almost all men under the age of forty-six at the time, or 24 million men. If you had a male ancestor who was between the ages of eighteen and forty-six at that time, the chances of finding him in draft records are very high. Draft registration cards varied over time but range in information from name and birthplace to the name of the individual's nearest relative and employer. Details could also include the registrant's age, employer information, physical description (including eye and hair color), and father's birthplace.

- Pension records—Originally granted to disabled soldiers and sailors, then to those who depended on the veteran, pensions were authorized after various wars, with different requirements depending on the war. To receive a pension, individuals had to apply, often with details such as marriage information and property schedules. Other details in pension records could include the name of the soldier, rank, and area of military service. While the average pension application was about thirty pages long, some were as long as two hundred pages. Pension records often include details about events that happened during the individual's service, relevant family letters, discharge papers, and marriage, birth, and death records.

- Veterans lists—Various veterans lists contain such information and records as newspaper articles, soldiers' ranks and assignments, letters sent from soldiers during the war, and grave site locations.

- Regimental histories—Read detailed accounts of a unit's participation in a war, often including names of commanders and other important men.

- Compiled service records—Compiled service records for various states contain a range of information gathered from various sources. They could include rosters with the full names of officers, non-commissioned officers, and privates. You can learn about an individual's rank, unit, date mustered in and out, medical information, and other details from the combined abstracts of muster rolls, pay vouchers, and more.

Where to begin

Before you begin researching your family history, start recording what you know. Did you have a parent who served in the U.S. military? How about a grandparent or an uncle? In which war did this individual serve? Write down any military facts you know or believe about family members. This will help you organize which wars you will want to research first for information about that ancestor.

Next, interview your family members. Ask them if they know of any ancestors who served in the military and see if they can tell you anything about those individuals' involvement with the wars.

Any details, even if they are small or if you cannot be sure about their accuracy, can help you narrow your research. You can confirm the details when you find military records about the ancestor.

Create a historical timeline and write down which individual served in the military in relation to which war. You can find a list of all the major wars and many of the smaller wars in which the United States was involved in this book.

You are looking for the answers to the following questions:

- Do you already know when and where in the armed forces he or she served? If so, did he or she serve in the enlisted ranks or was he or she an officer? If not, do you have family members who may have some information?

- When and where did the individual live?

- Did the family keep evidence of military service? Check for certificates, letters, journals, diaries, scrapbooks, newspaper clippings, photographs, medals, swords, and other memorabilia that may give you some background information.

- What are the known dates and places of residence of an individual from birth through adulthood? You may be able to narrow down an ancestor's participation in a war to regional conflicts in the ancestor's life.

This book is intended to help a newer researcher get a good start on their family history research with war records. To do so, make sure you know what you are looking for before you travel to libraries and archives. Also, find out the location's hours, including any special holiday hours.

Clues in non-military specific sources

In 2007, a street in Utah was named after a soldier who died in the Iraq war. As a result, post-death, the soldier received a lot of media attention that is now a part of each newspaper's permanent archives. This soldier may not be remembered on a nationwide level, but, as is the case with many towns, he will be recorded as a local hero.

Local histories, from newspaper archives to local history books, provide valuable details about military involvement. *A Bibliography of American County Histories* (Filby 1985) lists five thousand sources like these. Local public libraries and historical societies often collect and share other useful publications, including war memorabilia, biographies, letters, and journals.

Cemetery records often provide information about a soldier's rank and unit designation. In addition to standard cemeteries, the Department of Veterans Affairs National Cemetery Administration maintains military cemeteries in thirty-nine states. You can search for them at the following website: <http://gravelocator.cem. va.gov/j2ee/servlet/NGL_v1>. The Department of the Army and the National Park Service also maintain a few national cemeteries.

Depending on the year in which a census was conducted, some census records give details about an individual's military service. Censuses that recorded military details include the following:

- 1890—Special census recording Union veterans and widows of veterans, but names beginning with letters A through K were lost in a fire.

- 1900—Military schedules and indexes for military personnel, including U.S. bases overseas and navy (only) vessels.

- 1910—Census recording survivors of the Union or Confederate army or navy.

- 1920—Some but not all military bases in the United States. Some overseas military and naval forces were also recorded.

- 1930—Census indicating veterans, including what war or conflict they served in.

Some court records also detailed individuals who were discharged from the military. Also, because of legislation enacted in 1862, aliens over the age of twenty-one who had been honorably discharged from the United States military could qualify for naturalization. These records provide limited information but could provide enough clues to search military records that would provide more details.

Where to look in military records

Once you narrow down which ancestor served or may have served in a particular war, get some background information about the war and about what kinds of war records were developed as a result of that war. In the main portion of this book, you will find a section about each war that will give you background on the history of that particular war, followed by what records were developed as a result of that war and where you can go to obtain that information. The last section of each war lists databases available at Ancestry.com. Start with the materials available closest to you before traveling to further distances. The more material you have, the more success you can expect from your research trips to libraries, archives (specifically, the National Archives), and other research sites.

In addition to records that have been made available on the Internet and through research sites, do not forget published pieces, some of which are mentioned throughout this book. Some researchers may be lucky enough to find a collection of letters or a journal from one of their ancestors. In the Introduction to James C. Neagles's *U.S. Military Records*, Loretto Dennis Szucs shows the value of such records. On page 3, she quotes a collection of letters written by an eighteen-year-old soldier between December 1917 and November 1918.

The soldier writes "Somewhere in France" on his return envelopes. His letters must have been especially meaningful to his family, who never saw him alive again. One excerpt from his letters reads, "Well, I guess we got 'Jerry' on the run now and it won't be long before he will realize it. I came out of the trenches Sunday night and during the time I was in, I tried to make it as uncomfortable for him as I could." Szucs also talks about how even though the soldier died shortly after his last letter, we can fill in more of his story by looking for other information, like reading a history of his battalion or unit.

What you can find at Ancestry.com

ANCESTRY.COM HAS AN EXTENSIVE COLLECTION of military records, which continues to grow. The collection includes

more than 175 military collections covering a wide range of wars and conflicts, from some of the early Indian wars to the Vietnam War.

Below is a sampling of the types of databases included in the military collection at Ancestry.com:

- Lists of soldiers from various wars, sometimes for specific states

- Lists of officers from various wars, sometimes for specific states

- Navy and marine records

- Prisoner of war records for various wars

- Pension records

- State rosters

- Veterans lists

- Volunteer lists

- World War I and World War II draft cards

You can view all the military databases available in the Military Records Collection at Ancestry.com at <www.ancestry.com/search/rectype/default.aspx?rt=39>.

Please note, to search individual collections, you will want to scroll down to the section called "Search Individual Military Collections."

You can also find valuable military records, from photographs to personal stories, using the **Search** tab on Ancestry.com, at <www.ancestry.com/search/>.

Search the last two tabs, **Stories & Publications** and **Photos & Maps**, for user-submitted material, newspapers, historical stories, historical maps, and more details relating to war.

Military Records Center

Ancestry.com also provides a free online information center, called the Military Records Center, to assist researchers, at <www.ancestry.com/learn/contentcenters/contentCenter.aspx?page=military>.

The Military Records Center is a very basic tool but offers some general advice about what you can learn about individuals from military records, including updates on some of the newest records on Ancestry.com. The center also offers some details about types of military records available, interesting facts, frequently asked questions, and more.

This book is organized so each database that Ancestry.com offers, pertinent to that war, is listed with each war. This is meant to save individuals wasted trips to libraries and archives by ensuring they have all the facts they can gather online first, before making any trips.

Free, print-ready forms

Anyone that has ever looked at an original World War I Draft Registration Card, a census record, or some other form, knows that while these sources can provide very valuable, new information, there are some inherent difficulties. Since records were usually originally created for other purposes, and not for the long-term use of family history research, not all steps were taken to ensure the best preservation and readability of such records. Researchers have to interpret each individual's unique handwriting, in addition to trying to read the small description lines that have become blurred with the combination of age and preservation techniques.

Use the blank charts and forms at Ancestry. com <www.ancestry.com/trees/charts/ancchart. aspx?> alongside any records of interest to assist with interpreting lines.

About This Book

THE PURPOSE OF THIS BOOK is to help you locate what military records are available on Ancestry.com. The discussions of the wars and the other resources provided are meant to provide context for your search. Use this book as a starting point in your research.

AMERICAN WARS AND CONFLICTS

The Jamestown Conflicts, Virginia, 1622–44

THE FIRST WAR IN THE UNITED STATES happened only fifteen years after England's first permanent American colony took up residence in 1607. The settlers had chosen to settle along the James River because of its defensive position against enemies that might approach by water. Ironically, their problems were inland; an ongoing struggle with the Indians.

As the English attempted to expand their settlement, they encroached on Indian land, leading to continual conflict with the Indians. Finally, Chief Opechancanough led a surprise attack in 1622 on the English settlements. The attack resulted in 347 colonist deaths. The colonists responded with a counterattack, killing 250 Indians, most of whom were poisoned with liquor. In 1644, Opechancanough lead another attack, killing nearly 500 colonists. The chief was captured and killed during their final revolt that year.

Image from ClipArt.com

What records were generated because of the conflict

No records were specifically created for this conflict but because King James I ordered Virginia's leaders to take a census, deaths resulting from the attack were recorded. The 1623/4 census, known as a muster, includes names of individuals who survived the 1622 attack that killed 347 colonists. Ages and relationships were not recorded.

The musters listing colonists who died are searchable at <www.virtualjamestown.org/Muster/muster24. html>. The original 1623/4 and 1624/5 musters are in the Public Record Office in London, England.

In addition, the colonist Robert Beverley gives a firsthand account of the 1622 attack, biased toward the colonists, in *History and Present State of Virginia* (1705) at <www.virtualjamestown.org/1622attk.html>.

What you can find at Ancestry.com

Ancestry.com has a wealth of resources that encompass that period of time in Virginia. You may want to look into these online databases:

Maps of the original settlements in Virginia

www.ancestry.com/search/rectype/reference/maps/default.aspx

Virginia Land, Marriage, and Probate Records, 1639–1850

www.ancestry.com/search/db.aspx?dbid=7832

Passenger and Immigration Lists Index, 1500s-1900s
about Gabriel Archer

Name:	**Gabriel Archer**
Year:	1607
Place:	Jamestown, Virginia
Source Publication Code:	1219.4
Primary Immigrant:	Archer, Gabriel
Source Bibliography:	COLDHAM, PETER WILSON. The Complete Book of Emigrants: A Comprehensive Listing Compiled from English Public Records of Those Who Took Ship to the Americas for Political, Religious, and Economic Reasons; of Those Who Were Deported for Vagrancy, Roguery, or Non-Conformity; and of Those Who Were Sold to Labour in the New Colonies. Baltimore: Genealogical Publishing Co. 1607-1660. 1988. 600p.
Page:	1

Save This Record
Attach this record to a person in your tree as a source record, or save for later evaluation.

Save ▾

Source Citation: Place: *Jamestown, Virginia*; Year: *1607*; Page Number: *1*.

Passenger and Immigration Lists Index, 1500s–1900s

www.ancestry.com/search/db.aspx?dbid=7486

Virginia Immigrants, 1623–66

www.ancestry.com/search/db.aspx?dbid=2063

You can also view lists of names of early Jamestown inhabitants by visiting <www.rootsweb.com/~usgenweb/va/jamestown.htm>.

Pequot War, Connecticut, 1636–38

AS THE PURITAN COLONISTS IN NEW ENGLAND expanded their terrain, they came in contact with the Pequot tribe, which had recently established itself as the predominant tribe over other Indians in the Connecticut Valley.

The Pequots and Puritans signed a treaty in 1634 in an attempt at peace, but efforts failed. Several incidents occurred that eventually lead to war between the two groups. In these incidents, Puritans and Pequots were individually attacked and killed by small groups, sometimes in retaliation. For instance, Puritans held an Indian trader for ransom, then after the ransom was paid, returned the body, dead. Finally, on 26 May 1637, the Puritans attacked and killed an estimated six hundred Indians at the Pequots' fort on the Mystic River. The Puritans also burned down the village inside the fort. Most of the remaining Pequots were killed in 1638, including their chief, Sassascus.

The Treaty of Hartford, signed on 21 September 1638, disbanded the remaining members of the Pequot tribe, banishing them, often as slaves to other tribes that were allied with the Puritans.

What records were generated because of the conflict

No specific records were generated because of this war, but many references that mention it can be used to identify specific individuals associated with the Pequot War, such as *The Pequot War* by Alfred A. Cave.

What you can find at Ancestry.com

Ancestry.com has a wealth of resources that encompass that period of time in Connecticut. You may want to look into these online databases and resources:

Founders and Leaders of Connecticut, 1633–1783

http://content.ancestry.com/ iexec/?htx=BookList&dbid=16211

Pages 41, 42, 52, 91, and 92 of this book include names of individuals involved in the Pequot War.

Connecticut Puritan Settlers, 1633–1845

www.ancestry.com/search/db.aspx?dbid=4513

This collection lists many of the first settlers in Connecticut. The Pequot War is not specifically mentioned, but chances of overlap are strong.

Hartford County, Connecticut: Memorial History 1633–1884, Volume I–II

http://content.ancestry.com/ iexec/?htx=List&dbid=6549

This town history includes a section on the militia of Hartford County.

A catalogue of the names of the first Puritan settlers of the colony of Connecticut, **by Royal Ralph Hinman, published 1988, p. 91**

http://content.ancestry.com/browse/bookview.aspx?dbid=16187&iid=dvm_LocHist004143-00021-0&desc=King+William'S+War

This local history includes references to early settlers of Connecticut who were involved in the Pequot War:

Windsor—he built a house there, and afterwards gave one half of it to his son.) Mr. H. died n 1657. His widow married again. His children, Abigail, Joshua, Sarah, Benajah, Deborah, Nathaniel and Jonathan. His son Joshua married Ruth Stanwood in 1663, and had three children. Benajah married Sarah Eno, and had Benajah and James.—*Hayden. Record.*

Hull, George, Windsor—surveyed Wethersfield in 1636—deputy in April, August and September in '39—was a magistrate and member of the General Court often. He was allowed to trade for beaver on the river—was one of the Gen. Court that declared war against the Pequotts in '37 ; and he surveyed Windsor and Wethersfield by order of court the same year. He was a man of great worth in the colony.

Hull, John, married Elizabeth Loomis, of Windsor, in 1641. He came from Dorchester. A committee of the General Court in 1637-8-9.

Hull, Josiah, Hartford, 1640.

Hudson, or Hudgson, John, an atttorney at Hartford.

Hussey. Stephen. 1663.

King Philip's War, Massachusetts, Rhode Island, 1675–76

ALSO KNOWN AS THE GREAT INDIAN WAR OF 1675, King Philip's War is named after Metacomet (who was also known as King Philip), the son of the Wampanoag chief who led the destruction of white settlements throughout New England until his death in August 1676. This war is significant because it marked the almost complete loss of Indian land, which was awarded to colonial veterans of the war. This war was a turning point in which the colonists became the dominant force in the region.

The war was triggered by the execution of three Wampanoags for the murder of a Christian Indian, but according to many historians, the real issue was European encroachment and their treatment of the Indians. An angered King Philip led the Indians to destroy many white settlements throughout New England, including several thousand colonists and a dozen towns. The war ended when Philip was killed in August 1676.

What records were generated because of the conflict

Individuals involved in King Philip's War are listed at <www.usgennet.org/usa/topic/newengland/philip/>. These names were recorded by John Hull, treasurer-at-war of the Massachusetts Colony from 1675–78.

A search for "King Philip's War" at <http://books.google.com/> will also produce helpful results,

1636 - 1676

including several fully viewable digital books about King Philip's War. One of the digitized books lists the soldiers of Massachusetts Colony:

Bodge, George M. *Soldiers in King Philip's War: Being a Critical Account of That War, With a Concise History of the Indian Wars of New England From 1620–1677.* 3rd ed. Boston: the author, 1906. Reprint. Baltimore: Genealogical Publishing Co., 1976.

There are also some firsthand accounts of this war by Puritans, which are biased toward typically highly religious Puritans.

What you can find at Ancestry.com

Ancestry.com has a database that covers the military history of Watertown, including King Philip's War. For more information, visit the following:

Watertown, Massachusetts' Military History

http://content.ancestry.com/ iexec/?htx=List&dbid=8540

Watertown's Military History.

Name.	Town.
Wm White	Watertown
John Whitney	"
Saml Hinds	"
Charles Harrington	"
Nathl Harris	"
Henry Jipson	"
Joseph Palmer	Cambridge
Moses Souther	Watertown
Alexander Nelson	Cambridge
Ebenezer Fesandon	"
John Crane	Watertown
James Coollidge	"
Thaddeus Ward	"
Benjamin Learned	"
Joshua Stratton	"

Bacon's Rebellion, Virginia, 1676

ALSO KNOWN AS THE VIRGINIA REBELLION, Bacon's Rebellion is widely considered to be another territorial war, with colonists encroaching on more Indian land. However, this was also a war of discontent caused by economic problems.

The frontiersmen were unhappy that Royal Governor William Berkeley would not retaliate for unfriendly Indian encounters on frontier settlements. Many of the disgruntled colonists supported Nathaniel Bacon, who wanted to fight the Indians. When Berkeley had Bacon arrested, many colonists joined in to force his release. The majority of those rebelling were slaves, servants, and poor farmers. With his rebellious group, Bacon then formed a militia of five hundred men that massacred peaceful Indians.

Bacon continued to rise in power in the colony. He forced Berkeley to flee Jamestown, plundered and burned the community, and continued his rebellion until he died of dysentery on 26 October 1676. Berkeley returned with merchant ships and used their cannons and crews to end the rebellion. Many of the rebels were then hanged, while many more fled to North Carolina.

What records were generated because of the conflict

A record of Bacon's Rebellion is found in this account:

Neville, John D. comp. *Bacon's Rebellion: Abstracts of Materials in the Colonial Records Project.* Jamestown: Jamestown Foundation, 1976.

What you can find at Ancestry.com

One way to find records about Bacon's Rebellion is to go to the **Search** tab; click the **Stories & Publications** tab and perform a keyword search for "Bacon's Rebellion." On the search results page, click either "Early Settlers of Alabama," or "Old Virginia and her Neighbors."

Also, see the following databases:

Virginia Colonial Militia, 1651–1776
www.ancestry.com/search/db.aspx?dbid=4596

Virginia Colonial Soldiers
www.ancestry.com/search/db.aspx?dbid=4006

Virginia Biographical Encyclopedia
www.ancestry.com/search/db.aspx?dbid=4646

1675 - 1676

King George's War, Canada, Northern New England, New York, 1740–48

KNOWN IN EUROPEAN HISTORY as the War of the Austrian Succession, King George's War is the third of four European wars between England and France that culminated in the French and Indian War of 1754. During King George's War, France and England fought over the colonies, which led to the French attack on Port Royal, Nova Scotia, in 1744. However, the attack was unsuccessful.

On 18 April 1745, the preacher William Pepperell successfully led 4,200 volunteers along with an English fleet led by Sir Peter Warren to attack the powerful French stronghold Fort Louisburg in Canada. The city surrendered two months later.

However, French and Indian forces attacked and burned Saratoga, New York, after the English persuaded the Iroquois league to enter the war against the French.

King George's War ended when the Treaty of Aix-la-Chapelle was signed on 18 October 1748, restoring America to the same status it held before the war had begun. This war became a small truce in the scheme of the overall war between France and England.

What records were generated because of the conflict

As a result of the war, records were generated detailing who was called into the service, as well as who received pensions for veterans and widows.

RootsWeb.com has made available a list created in conjunction with the USGenWeb Archives Pension Project for the State of Virginia, which provides details on confederate pension rolls for veterans and widows of King George County. You can view this list at <http://ftp.rootsweb.com/pub/usgenweb/va/kinggeorge/military/civilwar/pensions/roles.txt>.

You may also want to visit the Massachusetts Archives located at the following address:

220 Morrissey Boulevard
(at Columbia Point, south of downtown Boston)
Boston, Massachusetts 02125
(617) 727-2816

Look for the following:

Lists of Men Who Served in British Military Organizations, 1710–74

Search for name, enlistment date, time in service, and amount of pay due. Check microfilm reels 91–99. There is an alphabetical name index on microfilm as well.

Government Responses to Petitions Claiming Remuneration for Military Service Rendered or for

Losses as a Result of Hostile Actions Against or by Indians, 1643–74

Each set of records is accompanied by a table of contents and a name index; available on microfilm reels 67–80 of Massachusetts Archives; arranged chronologically.

The Rhode Island Service, Muster Rolls, 1776–80

You may also want to look for this book:

Potter, Chandler E. *The Military History of the State of New Hampshire, 1623–1861, From Its Settlement, in 1623, to the Rebellion, in 1861…Biographical Notices of Many of the Officers…Concord: 1866 [1868].* Reprint "with added indexes…." Baltimore: Genealogical Publishing Co., 1972.

What you can find at Ancestry.com

The following is available on Ancestry.com concerning King George's War:

Rhode Island Privateers in King George's War

http://content.ancestry.com/ iexec/?htx=BookList&dbid=16527

The Rhode Island Colonial War Servicemen, 1740– 62

www.ancestry.com/search/db.aspx?dbid=4055

Rhode Island Colonial War Servicemen, 1740-62
about John A. MORRILL

Given Name:	**John A.**
Surname:	**MORRILL**
War Served In:	King George's War
Notes:	Quartermaster on Privateer Charming Betty in 1744.

Save This Record
Attach this record to a person in your tree as a source record, or save for later evaluation.

Save ▾

French and Indian War, Northern Colonies and Canada, 1754–63

THE FRENCH AND INDIAN WAR started in America then spread to Europe. The war was a battle between France and England, each country seeking complete rule over North America and each country having placed settlers from their countries in America. While the battle was between France and England, the war is known as the French and Indian War because the French and Indians were allied against the English. This war was significant because it determined who would shape America—the French or the English. The aftereffects of the expensive war would also lead the British to tax the English colonists, which in turn lead to the Revolutionary War.

In Quebec and other parts of Canada, the French and Indian War is known best as the War of the Conquest because the British conquered New France and made it part of the British Empire. The Europeans know the war as the Seven Years' War because of the length of the war. For the colonists, the war began in 1754, when border disputes led to the first battle over what is now Pittsburgh. At that time, a twenty-two-year-old Lt. Col. George Washington led 150 men against French who were trespassing on their Virginia territory. The English colonists were defeated by nine hundred Frenchmen, who sent Washington back to Virginia rather than killing him.

Though the English colonists outnumbered the French, the French were better fighters and were allied with the Indians. The Indians may have had numerous reasons for choosing the French as allies over the English, but the most obvious one is the years of battle and destruction they had already endured from the English colonists. Though the French were largely winning the battles, one significant moment for family historians was when British naval forces took over Nova Scotia and exiled the French, who were known as the Acadians. The Acadians largely traveled down to Louisiana; their descendants are known today as Cajuns.

France and England officially declared war on 15 May 1756. The majority of the fighting occurred in the Great Lakes area. The French were winning the war until William Pitt was put in charge of the English battles and changed their war strategy to focus on naval warfare. In other significant moments in the war, Louisburg was captured in 1759, and the British took the Canadian empire from France in 1760 when the Marquis de Vaudreuil surrendered Montreal.

On 10 February 1763, the French and English agreed to the Treaty of Paris. France lost a great deal of land, giving all of Canada to Britain except two small islands off Newfoundland.

What records were generated because of the conflict

The English government kept records of state militia organi-zations that they paid to fight in the Indian Wars from 1790 until 1796, including muster records and payrolls of the state militia troops. As a result, there are several publications available that list names of individuals involved in the French and Indian War, as gleaned from these records.

For instance, the following publication lists names of individuals involved in the French and Indian War:

Taylor, Philip F. *A Calendar of the Warrants for Land in Kentucky, Granted for Service in the French and Indian War.* Baltimore: Genealogical Publishing Co., 1967.

You may also want to visit the Pennsylvania State Archives at the following address:

> P.O. Box 1026
> Third and Forster Streets
> Harrisburg, Pennsylvania, 17108-1026
> (717) 783-3281

Though according to the Pennsylvania State Archives online at <www.phmc.state.pa.us/Bah/DAM/military/fiwar.htm>, their original documentation of service in the French and Indian War is limited, you can look for twenty muster rolls and military returns. These records are filed under *Papers of the Provincial Council, 1682–1775*

(Record Group, or RG, 21). The Pennsylvania State Archives also have some historical records pertaining to the war in Manuscript Group 7, 8, 19, 30, 125, 193, and 382.

In addition, look for *Guide to the Manuscript Groups in the Pennsylvania State Archives*, edited by Harry E. Whipkey (Harrisburg: Pennsylvania Historical and Museum Commission) for military units, prisoner-of-war lists, and more.

Also, visit the Virginia State Library and Archives:

> Eleventh Street at Capitol Square
> Richmond, Virginia 23219
> (804) 786-8929

Look for the Colonial Wars section. The Military Accounts Ledger, 1762–84 (microfilm) lists accounts of expenses during the French and Indian War— principally pensions to disabled soldiers and their widows.

The Massachusetts Archives Collection Database (1629–1799) at <www.sec.state.ma.us/ArchivesSearch/RevolutionarySearch.aspx> also includes the French and Indian War.

The British government also recruited many individuals from Scotland for the French and Indian War, and there are specific records available just about Scottish soldiers.

1754 – 1763

23

What you can find at Ancestry.com

The following resources are available at Ancestry.com:

American Militia in the Frontier Wars, 1790–1796

http://content.ancestry.com/
iexec/?htx=BookList&dbid=49028

This is an online book consisting of the records of state militia organizations the government used to fight in the Indian Wars.

Rhode Island Colonial War Servicemen, 1740–62

www.ancestry.com/search/db.aspx?dbid=4055

Connecticut Soldiers, French and Indian War, 1755–62

www.ancestry.com/search/db.aspx?dbid=3983

Scottish Soldiers in Colonial America, Part Three

http://content.ancestry.com/
iexec/?htx=BookList&dbid=49348

This database includes the time of arrival of Scottish soldiers who joined the American colonies, as well as the civilian occupations they took as they became integrated into the colonies.

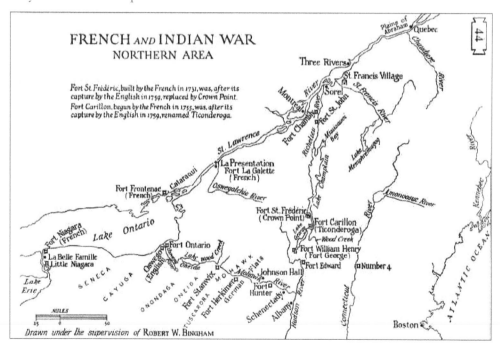

The French and Indian War from Scottish Sources

http://content.ancestry.com/
iexec/?htx=BookList&dbid=49162

To view more resources related to the French and Indian War, go to the Ancestry.com **Search** tab at <www.ancestry.com/search/>, then under "Search Records," click the **Photos & Maps** tab. In the "Keywords" field, enter "French and Indian War." This will produce results for both photographs and maps relating to this war, like the one shown on the previous page.

Pontiac's Rebellion, Michigan, New York, Pennsylvania, 1763–66

AFTER THE FRENCH AND INDIAN WAR ENDED, the Indians were forced to trade with the British instead of the French, which they did not like because of British trading practices. Chief Pontiac, an Ottawa Indian, attempted to drive the British out of the west in 1763 by mass attacking Fort Detroit in May, then raiding English settlements in Ohio and Pennsylvania. This led to the capture and death of over six hundred people. However, Colonel Henry Bouquet and Colonel John Bradstreet retaliated with invasions that stopped Chief Pontiac's attempts and led to a peace treaty in 1766.

What records were generated because of the conflict
No known records were found for this conflict.

What you can find at Ancestry.com
In the U.S. Map Collection, search for Pontiac War in the "Map Title" field and you will see several maps detailing the area in which the war took place.
www.ancestry.com/search/rectype/reference/maps/default.aspx

1754 – 1766

Lord Dunmore's War, Virginia, Pennsylvania, Ohio, 1773–74

LORD DUNMORE'S WAR WAS ANOTHER territory-related battle, resulting from British colonists moving onto Indian hunting ground south of the Ohio River, in what is now West Virginia and Kentucky.

Tensions between the Indians and colonists were high, and many panicked colonists believed war was inevitable. Then, an Indian chief's family was murdered. The Indians retaliated until the Earl of Dunmore, John Murray, led a victorious attack against the Indians in the Battle of Point Pleasant on 10 October 1774, thus ending the war.

What records were generated because of the conflict

Few records exist for Lord Dunmore's War, but the Virginia State Library and Archives has some information at their location at the following address:

> Eleventh Street at Capitol Square
> Richmond, Virginia 23219
> (804) 786 – 8929

Look in the Colonial Wars index for Dunmore's War. This is a card index that will include name, county, unit, and source reference information.

What you can find at Ancestry.com

In the U.S. Map Collection, search for "War" and type in "Mid-Atlantic States" in the "Area" field. The second map you see is a map of Dunmore's War, like that shown here.

www.ancestry.com/search/rectype/reference/maps/default.aspx

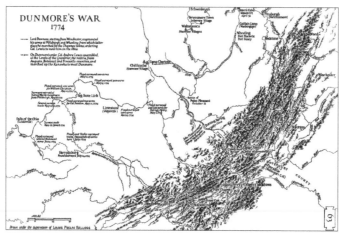

American Revolutionary War, American Colonies, 1775–83

ALSO KNOWN AS THE AMERICAN WAR OF INDEPENDENCE, the American Revolutionary War was a fight by the thirteen colonies of America for independence from Great Britain. Though several factors may have affected the colonists' desire for independence, Britain's attempt to tax the colonists ultimately led to revolution.

Britain's main reason for taxing the colonists was their attempt to recover the costs of the French and Indian War. However, the colonists were offended at being taxed from across the ocean when they were not represented in Parliament. The issue of taxation escalated, resulting in boycotts. The situation grew worse when Britain sent 4,000 British soldiers to Boston (population 16,000), adding job competition and increased resentment.

Finally, the colonists dumped tea off a British boat rather than paying taxes for the tea. After this act of rebellion, called the Boston Tea Party, the British closed the port and fined the colonists, who never paid. Similar "tea parties" were held, and the British responded by sending troops. In the meantime, the colonies had their own troops, resulting from militias that were formed originally for protection against Indian attacks. The colonies' Continental Army was lead by Virginian General George Washington and consisted of individuals from every colony. The colony also had a Continental Navy, as well as militia and colonial troops for individual colonies.

On 18 April 1775, Paul Revere received the warning that the British were crossing the Charles River in boats and sounded a warning. In "the shot heard round the world," the following day, British soldiers sent to arrest Samuel Adams and John Hancock ended up killing eight minutemen when an unauthorized gunshot caused chaos between the two groups.

Following this event, the colonies succeeded in capturing Fort Ticonderoga in May, and then seriously hurt British troops during the battle of Bunker Hill on 17 June 1775.

On 7 June 1776, the Second Continental Congress issued the Declaration of Independence, whose original draft was authored by Thomas Jefferson.

1773 - 1783

On 17 October 1777, the colonists trapped the British army in New York, at which point the French became involved, lending money and gunpowder to the colonists. The French support gave the colonists the edge they needed to win the war. On 19 October 1781, the colonists and French armies trapped General Lord Cornwallis in Yorktown, and he subsequently surrendered. The Treaty of Paris brought an end to the war on 3 September 1783. The treaty was ratified by Congress in January 1784.

What records were generated because of the conflict

After the American Revolutionary War, bounty lands were rewarded to individuals for services rendered during the war. Each of the nine state governments kept its own records for lands rewarded in that region, including the name and rank of the individuals.

Records were also kept listing mariners, loyalists, and other soldiers of the American Revolution, as well as courts-martial, pensions, land grants, and more. The 1840 U.S. Federal Census recorded the names and ages of all individuals who served in the Revolutionary War living at that time.

You may want to visit the National Archives:

> The National Archives
> Pennsylvania Avenue NW
> Washington, D.C.

At the National Archives, you can find many records regarding regular army officers and enlisted men in the National Archives publication Preliminary Inventory Number 17, *Records of the Adjutant General's Office*. This publication also references other useful sources listing regular army and navy officers, especially William H. Powell's *List of Officers of the Army of the United States From 1779 to 1900*. Also, look for Francis B. Heitman's *Historical Register of the Officers of the Continental Army During the War of the Revolution*.

The following microfilm may be helpful to you:

* *General Index to Compiled Service Records of Revolutionary War Soldiers* (M860).

* *General Index to Compiled Service Records of American Naval Personnel Who Served During the Revolutionary War* (M879).

* *Revolutionary War Rolls, 1775–1783* (M246).

* *Index to Compiled Service Records of Revolutionary War Soldiers Who Served with the American Army in Connecticut Military Organizations* (M920).

* *Index to Compiled Service Records of Revolutionary War Soldiers Who Served with the American Army in Georgia Military Organizations* (M1051).

* *Selected Records from the Revolutionary War Pension and Bounty Land Warrant Application Files, 1800–1900* (M805).

* *Miscellaneous Numbered Records (the Manuscript File) in the War Department Collection of Revolutionary War Records, 1775–1790s* (M859—32 reels).

You can also search the National Archives online database for some pension and bounty-land war applications related to the Revolutionary War by visiting <http://arcweb.archives.gov/arc/basic_search.jsp>. Be sure to check the box under the filter that says

"Descriptions of Archival Materials linked to digital copies."

Also, at the National Archives Military Reference Branch, look for the following:

RG 93—War Department Collection of Revolutionary War Records

The Library of Congress does not hold original military documents but can provide additional useful information, including the following:

Sellers, John R., et al. *Manuscript Sources in the Library of Congress for Research on the American Revolution.* Washington, D.C.: Library of Congress, 1975.

You can find a list of close to two hundred publications, guides, and bibliographies that pertain to the American Revolutionary War, including pensioners and bounty land recipients, in James C. Neagles' book, *U.S. Military Records*, pages 372–380.

In addition, The US GenWeb Archives is progressing on the US GenWeb Archives Pension Project to collect and share actual transcriptions from pension records and related pension materials. Many Revolutionary War pensioners are already listed in this project at <www.rootsweb.com/%7Eusgenweb/pensions/revwar/index.htm>.

Many of the state archives hold original records that give details about individuals who served in the American Revolutionary War. Some of the archives with the greatest wealth of information regarding this war include the following:

The Massachusetts Archives
220 Morrissey Boulevard
Boston, Massachusetts 02125
(617) 727-2816

The New Hampshire State Archives
Seventy-one South Fruit Street
Concord, New Hampshire 03301
(603) 271-2236

The New Jersey State Archives
185 West State Street
CN-307
Trenton, New Jersey 08625
(609) 292-6260

The Pennsylvania State Archives
P.O. Box 1026
Third and Forster Streets
Harrisburg, Pennsylvania, 17108-1026
(717) 783-3281

The Rhode Island State Archives
337 Westminster Street
Providence, Rhode Island 02903-3302
(401) 277-2353

What you can find at Ancestry.com

You can find the following on Ancestry.com:

Mariners of the American Revolution

http://content.ancestry.com/
iexec/?htx=BookList&dbid=49233

This book lists thousands of captured American privateers, the names of their ships, the dates of their confinement, and more.

Loyalists in the American Revolution: Miscellaneous Records

www.ancestry.com/search/db.aspx?dbid=6134

Massachusetts Soldiers and Sailors in the War of the Revolution, 17 Vols.

www.ancestry.com/search/db.aspx?dbid=3090

Muster and Pay Rolls of the War of the Revolution, 1775–1783: Miscellaneous Records

www.ancestry.com/search/db.aspx?dbid=6154

Revolutionary War Bounty Land Grants

http://content.ancestry.com/
iexec/?htx=BookList&dbid=49315

Bounty lands awarded to citizens and soldiers for services rendered.

Revolutionary War Courts-Martial

www.ancestry.com/search/db.aspx?dbid=1045

Lists over 3,000 soldiers.

Revolutionary War Officers

www.ancestry.com/search/db.aspx?dbid=2030

Revolutionary War Pension Index

www.ancestry.com/search/db.aspx?dbid=4691

Revolutionary War Pensioner Census, 1841

http://content.ancestry.com/
iexec/?htx=List&dbid=7678

Revolutionary War Service Records, 1775–83

www.ancestry.com/search/db.aspx?dbid=4282

American Revolutionary War Rejected Pensions

www.ancestry.com/search/db.aspx?dbid=4329

Fire Cake and Water

http://content.ancestry.com/
iexec/?htx=BookList&dbid=49154

This is a book about the Continental Army at Valley Forge.

What Can't Brave Americans Endure

http://content.ancestry.com/
iexec/?htx=BookList&dbid=49395

This is a book about the Continental Army at Valley Forge.

You can find photos and maps of the American Revolution, like the map shown here from the U.S. Map Collection, 1513–1990 by searching for "American Revolution" under the **Photos & Maps** tab at <www.ancestry.com/search/>.

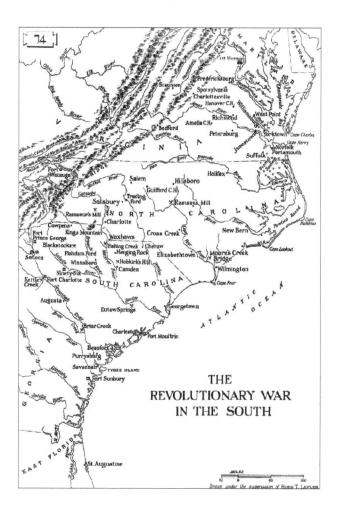

THE
REVOLUTIONARY WAR
IN THE SOUTH

Shays' Rebellion, Massachusetts, 1786–87

THE MASSACHUSETTS LEGISLATURE would not listen to the needs of destitute farmers seeking financial help. The farmers were faced with a cycle of poverty and taxes that seemed insurmountable since many did not fulfill the requirements of owning property and therefore could not vote.

Captain Daniel Shays led a group of farmers from western Massachusetts against merchants and lawyers, demanding that debtors no longer be indicted by courts. Though the rebels grew to as many as one thousand, they did not have enough power to win a battle. However, a new legislature, elected within the year, addressed some of the farmers' hardships. More attention was paid to the value of an effective central government, too.

What records were generated because of the conflict

Some muster records were kept that reflect some of the individuals involved in Shays' Rebellion.

The Massachusetts Archives has microfilm about these muster records at the following address:

220 Morrissey Boulevard
(at Columbia Point, south of downtown Boston)
Boston, Massachusetts 02125
(617) 727-2816

Look for the following:

Muster Rolls and Certificates of Service, Shays' Rebellion, 1787 (microfilm)

What you can find at Ancestry.com

There are no records currently available on Ancestry.com. If you're interested in records about Shays' Rebellion, check back frequently because it is likely Ancestry.com will digitize relevant records in the future.

1775 - 1787

Whiskey Rebellion, Pennsylvania, 1794

THE WHISKEY REBELLION IS SOMETIMES also called the Whiskey Insurrection. When the federal government placed an excise tax on whiskey in 1791, some of the more financially burdened families could not or would not pay the tax. They were required to appear in court in Philadelphia or New York. This trip often financially ruined an already burdened family. In 1794, counties in Pennsylvania rebelled. The new federal government responded by sending in the military to make some arrests. However, most cases were pardoned or dismissed.

What records were generated because of the conflict

You can visit the Pennsylvania Archives online at <www. digitalarchives.state.pa.us/archive.asp> (scroll to the bottom of the page and click "Militia Officers Index Cards, 1775–1800, series #13.36") to search or browse for Pennsylvania militia officers who participated in ending the Whiskey Rebellion. You can browse by letter, organized alphabetically by last name, or enter a name in the search field. Details may include name, county, rank, company, dates of service, and township.

You may also want to contact the Pennsylvania State Archives at the following address:

> P.O. Box 1026
> Third and Forster Streets
> Harrisburg, Pennsylvania, 17108-1026
> (717) 783-3281

Look for the following:

Pennsylvania Archives: 2nd ser., vol. 4; 4th ser., vol.4; 9th ser., vol. 2

Western Expedition Accounts, 1794–1804

You may also want to visit the New Jersey Historical Society at the following address:

> 52 Park Place
> Newark, New Jersey 07102
> (973) 596-8500 x249

The New Jersey Historical Society provides personal papers related to the Whiskey Rebellion at the following Web address: <www.jerseyhistory.org/arch_military. html>. Click on the links corresponding to the rebellion to find details about the individual who wrote the paper, his involvement with the Whiskey Rebellion, and the collection number to find the paper when visiting.

What you can find at Ancestry.com

You can find the following on Ancestry.com:

American Militia in the Frontier Wars, 1790–1796

http://content.ancestry.com/
iexec/?htx=BookList&dbid=49028

Although this book focuses on the records of the state militia organizations that the government paid to fight in the Indian Wars from 1790 until 1796, it also contains valuable information on some of the militia troops that were sent to end the Whiskey Rebellion, such as the portion of the list shown in the following:

CHAPTER 5

NEW JERSEY MILITIA

Brigadier General A. White's Battalion

Captain Abram Shaver's Troop

Muster Roll of a Troop of Volunteer Light Dragoons Under the Command of Captain Abram Shaver in the Service of the United States Commanded by Brigadier General A. White from New Jersey during the Whiskey Insurrection from Sept 11 to Dec 1, 1794

Nr	Rank	Name	Remarks
1	Captain	Shaver, Abraham	commissioned Sept 11
2	Lieutenant	Beardslee, John	" " "
3	Cornet	Harriot, Sidney	" " "
4	Sergeant	Johnson, Jonathan	prom to Qtr Mstr Sergt Sept 16, discharged Oct 27
5	"	Harriot, Nathaniel	discharged Oct 12
6	"	Buckley, Robert	
7	"	Prigmore, Joseph	enlisted Sept 15 mustered under Lieut Potts promoted to Qtr Mstr Sergt Oct 27

War of 1812, Great Lakes, Maryland, New Orleans, 1812–15

ON 18 JUNE 1812, AN OUTRAGED AMERICA declared war on Great Britain. British naval vessels were essentially kidnapping American sailors and forcing them into the British navy under the authority of Great Britain. They forced thousands of sailors into British service. Americans were also unhappy that the British were restricting their trade while England fought with France. When America declared war, the British North American colonies and parts of Canada sided with Great Britain against America.

The American militias were unsuccessful at first, failing in their attempts to conquer Canada because of incompetence and lack of finances. In addition, the British created a naval blockade of Chesapeake and Delaware bays in 1812, which badly hurt American exporting but also benefited Americans by forcing them to rely on themselves for goods they previously imported.

Americans had time to become much better fighters while Britain was forced to allocate their most experienced veterans to defeating Napoleon's forces in France. Ironically, though Americans had become much

better fighters by the time Britain defeated France in 1814, the end of the war with France also eliminated most of the reasons America was even at war with Britain. The British impressments of American soldiers and the trade restrictions were both in place because of the war with France.

The two nations agreed to the Treaty of Ghent in 1815, which basically left the terms of Treaty of Paris, ignoring the issues that had arisen to cause the War of 1812, since the defeat of France had made the issues moot.

Unfortunately, some British troops and American militia did not hear about the treaty in time, and in the Battle of New Orleans, the British attacked the Americans and lost two thousand soldiers to America's eight.

What records were generated because of the conflict

The government kept federal service records for the War of 1812. There are also many compiled service records for the War of 1812, arranged by state or territory. These records include details on the Rangers put together to guard the frontier, the volunteer units developed to fight the British, and new units in both the army and navy. Other records cover state militias, volunteer army units, and other units involved in the war. There are also prisoner of war records that the Treasury Department and the Department of the Navy recorded and sent to the

Office of the Adjutant General. Also, look for bounty land grants awarded to veterans and pension benefits granted to heirs of veterans.

You will find a wealth of information at the following:

The National Archives
Pennsylvania Avenue NW
Washington, D.C.

Though the process may take months, you can also order copies of unrestricted military records by mail for a fee. To learn more about how to make a mail request, visit <www.archives.gov/veterans/military-service-records/standard-form-180.html>.

The following microfilm in the National Archives Microfilm Series will be helpful in your research:

* *Index to Compiled Service Records of Volunteer Soldiers Who Served During the War of 1812* (M602). You can find separate indexes to Mississippi (M678), Louisiana (M229), North Carolina (M220), and South Carolina (M652).

* *Index to War of 1812 Pension Application Files* (M313).

* *War of 1812 Military Bounty Land Warrants, 1815– 1858* (M848).

* *War of 1812 Papers of the Department of State, 1789–1815* (M588). These papers include lists of prisoners of war.

- *Despatches From United States Consuls in London, 1790–1906* (T168). Details include lists of prisoners of war.

- *Computer-processed Tabulations of Data From Seamen's Protective Certificate Applications to the Collector of Customs for the Port of Philadelphia, 1812–1815* (M972). Find information about sailors as described in certificates issued to prove U.S. citizenship during the War of 1812.

In addition to the main National Archives location, the National Archives also has many reference branches. One branch, RG-94—Adjutant General's Office, 1780s–1917, contains a useful record detailing rolls for state militia and other volunteer organizations, alphabetically by state: Muster Rolls of Volunteer Organizations: War of 1812, 1812–15.

The US GenWeb Archives Pension Project is collecting and sharing actual transcriptions from pension records and related pension materials that were developed because of the war. You can view names that are already listed by state, as well as contact a volunteer to become involved in the project at <www.rootsweb. com/%7Eusgenweb/pensions/1812/>.

There are several other locations holding historical accounts and records of the War of 1812, including the following:

U.S. Army Heritage and Education Center
950 Soldiers Drive
Carlisle, PA 17013
(717) 245-3971
<www.carlisle.army.mil/ahec/>

Maryland Historical Society
201 West Monument Street
Baltimore, Maryland 21201
(410) 685-3750

Massachusetts Archives
220 Morrissey Boulevard
Boston, Massachusetts 02125
(617) 727-2816
<www.sec.state.ma.us/arc/arcgen/genidx.htm>

What you can find at Ancestry.com

You can find the following at Ancestry.com:

War of 1812 Service Records

www.ancestry.com/search/db.aspx?dbid=4281

Compiled service records taken from the National Archives.

Louisiana Soldiers in the War of 1812

www.ancestry.com/search/db.aspx?dbid=3339

Pennsylvania Volunteers in the War of 1812

www.ancestry.com/search/db.aspx?dbid=3325

War of 1812: Miscellaneous Canadian Records

www.ancestry.com/search/db.aspx?dbid=6151

Includes information on Canadians and British, ranging from prisoners taken at Newark, property losses, volunteers, a pay list, muster rolls, a list of widows, and pension records.

Military Records: War of 1812 Muster Rolls

http://shops.ancestry.com/product.asp?productid=2019&shopid=126&catid=453

U.S. Map Collection, 1513–1990

http://content.ancestry.com/Browse/list.aspx?dbid=8739&path=

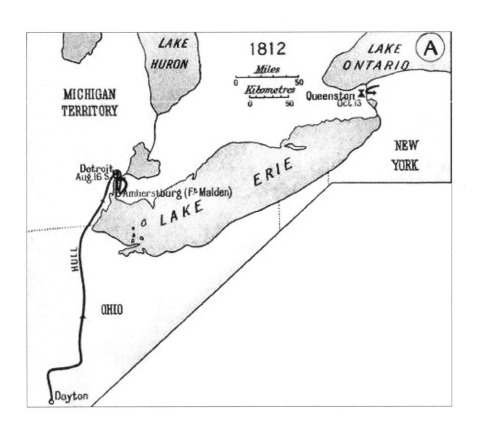

Indian Wars, 1811–1900

THE INDIAN WARS WERE A SERIES OF CONFLICTS between whites and Indians. There are many individual wars within the Indian Wars that are well known. Before the Civil War, these wars included the First Seminole War, Second Seminole War, and Third Seminole War in Florida; the Black Hawk War in Illinois and Wisconsin; the Navajo Wars in New Mexico and Arizona; and the Yakima Wars in Washington, Oregon, and Idaho. During the wars, the government forced most of the Indians in the southeast to what is now Oklahoma.

Another particularly famous war from this time was the Cherokee War, from 1759–61, in which about 17,000 Cherokees in the western United States were forced to relocate at gunpoint by 7,000 soldiers. The Cherokees covered 1,200 miles. The relocation, called the Trail of Tears, and led to an estimated 4,000 Cherokee deaths along the way.

In the Battle of Tippecanoe of 1811, the governor of the Indiana Territory built a fort near Tippecanoe Creek, with plans to meet with the hostile Chief Tenskwatawa. He brought 300 soldiers and 650 militiamen with him, who were attacked by the Indians on the day of the conference. Governor William Henry Harrison responded by burning the Indian village.

After the Civil War, the U.S. Army wanted more power to ensure that Indians who had been pushed off their land and onto reservations stayed on their reservations. At that time, there were still almost one hundred tribes in the Rocky Mountain region and in the Great Plains, along the route that settlers traveled. Over a thousand battles were waged between the Americans and the Indians, with the Indians being forced back onto their reservations time after time.

In the Sioux and Cheyenne Wars, the Sioux were forced onto reservations. Although the Sioux stayed on their reservations, white prospectors broke their agreement with the Sioux, so the Sioux fought back, successfully at first. On 29 December 1890, a group of two hundred Sioux men, women, and children left the reservation and were massacred in Wounded Knee, South Dakota.

In the Apache Wars, the Apaches resisted efforts to keep them on reservations in the Arizona area. One famous Indian, Geronimo, was an Apache who led raids after Mexican soldiers killed his family. He was later captured in Florida.

The Modoc War was the last Indian war in California. It occurred because the Modoc Indians were forced to share a reservation with rival Indians, the Klamaths, who harassed them. When the Modoc Indians attempted to leave, some Indians were hanged as punishment, and they were forced back onto the reservation.

In the Nez Perce Wars, the Indians traveled over 1,000 miles in three months to escape to Canada. They were running from nearly 2,000 U.S. soldiers. Only a small group of the Indians made it over the border before Chief Joseph surrendered. They were sent back to reservations in Idaho and Washington.

What records were generated because of the conflict

The original pension records relating to the Indian Wars are located at the National Archives. The series of pension files for military personnel who participated in the Indian Wars includes personal history questionnaires, such as spouse information.

The government compiled service records for this period. In addition, pensions were authorized for those who served in the military during this time frame. The original files are available at the National Archives.

You can also see a list of army casualties from the Second Seminole War in the following publication:

Bowden, J.J. *The Ponce de Leon Land Grant*. El Paso: Texas Western Press, 1969.

A work in progress, the US GenWeb Archives is progressing on the US GenWeb Archives Pension Project to collect and share actual transcriptions from pension records and related pension materials. Some Indian War pension records are already listed at < www.rootsweb.com/%7Eusgenweb/pensions/indian/ >.

What you can find at Ancestry.com

You will find the following specific databases and resources at Ancestry.com, or you can search for "Indian Wars" on either the **Stories & Publications** tab or the **Photos & Maps** tab. Select 1865 to 1900 as the time frame to narrow the search. The following image is an example of what you might find:

Dawes Commission Index, 1896
www.ancestry.com/search/db.aspx?dbid=3075
This database records 14,000 members the Five Civilized Tribes who applied for citizenship under the Act of 1896.

Dawes Commission Index, 1898–1914
www.ancestry.com/search/db.aspx?dbid=3118

Walker River Valley, Nevada Paiute Indian Records, 1897–1901

www.ancestry.com/search/db.aspx?dbid=3698

These reservation census records include name, gender, age, relationship to head of household, and year of census for more than twenty-five hundred residents.

Searching for Your American Indian Ancestors

www.ancestry.com/learn/library/article. aspx?article=5601

This 2002 article published by *Ancestry* Magazine provides helpful information on researching American Indian ancestors.

War of Texas Independence, Texas, 1836

IN 1836, THE REPUBLIC OF MEXICO included present-day Texas. At that time, Mexico offered Americans large tracts of land to settle in their territory. Soon, there were 30,000 Americans in Texas. When Mexico tried to impose laws over the Americans, the Americans declared independence on 2 March 1836. This led to the massacre at the Alamo where Davy Crockett, among two hundred other Americans, was killed, and more than one thousand Mexicans. When the president of Mexico was captured, he agreed to support an independent Texas, but he didn't keep his promise, resulting in a future war with Mexico.

What records were generated because of the conflict

A work in progress, the US GenWeb Archives is progressing on the US GenWeb Archives Pension Project to collect and share actual transcriptions from pension records and related pension materials that were developed because of the war. You can view names that are already available, as well as contact a volunteer to become involved in the project at <www.rootsweb. com/%7Eusgenweb/pensions/texrev/index.htm>.

What you can find at Ancestry.com

There are no records currently available on Ancestry. com. If you are interested in records about the War of Texas Independence, check back frequently because it is likely Ancestry.com will digitize relevant records in the future.

1811 - 1900

Aroostook War, Maine, 1839

THE AROOSTOOK WAR IS KNOWN BY MANY NAMES, including the Northeastern Boundary Dispute. The Treaty of Paris of 1783 left the boundary between New Brunswick and Maine unclear. This caused boundary disputes since New Brunswick was British and Maine was American. When Maine became a state in 1820, it began granting land used by Canadians in the valley of the Aroostook River to American settlers.

Maine prepared to back their promise to the settlers with as many as ten thousand Maine militiamen, but Britain and America were able to agree to a boundary commission in the Webster-Ashburton Treaty of 1842 without drawing blood.

What records were generated because of the conflict

Look for lists of volunteer's name, rank, and date of discharge, and information about drafts and payroll at the Maine State Archives:

> Cultural Building
> State House Station 84
> Augusta, Maine 04333-0084
> (207) 287-5790

Maine records for the Aroostook War include the following:

- Aroostook War Vouchers, Secretary of State
- Aroostook War Records in Land Office—civil posse
- Aroostook War Drafted Militia, 1839 (indexed)
- Muster Rolls and Payrolls, 1839

While the Aroostook War is known as a war where no blood was shed, there were some incidental deaths. You can view a list of the deaths at <http://members.tripod.com/~Scott_Michaud/Aroostook-War.html>.

What you can find at Ancestry.com

You can find the following at Ancestry.com:

About Aroostook War (Maine) History and Roster
www.ancestry.com/search/db.aspx?dbid=4518

Mexican War, Mexico, Texas, New Mexico, California, 1846–48

IN 1846, AMERICA BEGAN A WAR WITH MEXICO over territorial expansion. President Polk initially sent thousands of soldiers to guard what he considered to be America's borders from the War of Texas Independence of 1836. After some U.S. soldiers were killed, Polk declared war on Mexico. America invaded Mexico on September 1846, easily claiming victories in each battle with Mexico. The war ended with the Treaty of Guadalupe-Hidalgo, which formed the Rio Grande River as the official border between Texas and Mexico and also gave California and New Mexico to the United States. The treaty was signed on 2 February 1848.

What records were generated because of the conflict

A work in progress, the US GenWeb Archives is progressing on the US GenWeb Archives Pension Project to collect and share actual transcriptions from pension records and related pension materials that were developed because of the war. For more information, visit <www.rootsweb.com/%7Eusgenweb/pensions/mexwar/index.htm>.

What you can find at Ancestry.com

There are no records currently available on Ancestry.com. If you are interested in records about the Mexican War, check back frequently because it is likely Ancestry.com will digitize relevant records in the future.

1839 - 1848

Utah War, Utah, 1857–58

THE UTAH WAR WAS A RESULT OF SUSPICION toward members of The Church of Jesus Christ of Latter-day Saints, known as the Mormons. Faced with persecution, the Mormons had moved several times, finally settling in the Great Salt Lake Valley.

After Utah gained territorial status in 1850, the Mormons were accused of being disloyal to the United States. In what is called "Buchanan's Blunder," President James Buchanan declared Utah in rebellion without verifying details and sent troops to Utah.

He also failed to notify President Brigham Young of the Mormon church that he had sent Alfred Cumming to take his place as territorial governor. President Young willingly allowed Cumming to take that role.

However, responding to past persecution and with troops in their territory, President Young sent thirty thousand Mormons south to present-day Provo, Utah, in a mass migration. In the end, the troops that had been sent to Salt Lake City established a permanent base until the Civil War began.

What records were generated because of the conflict

Visit the Utah State Archives to research their large collection of military records, including those of the original territorial militia.

The Utah State Archives lists many of their resources online at <www.archives.state.ut.us/main/>.

LATER FROM SALT LAKE.

Memorial From the Legislature to Congress.

Mormon Harangues in the Tabernacle.

Brigham Still Determined to Rebel.

We have received, by way of California, files of the *Deseret News* to the 7th of January inclusive.

It is reported that BRIGHAM YOUNG has been instigating the Oregon Indians to rebel. He has offered to pay them a certain sum per head for every horse or mule they may capture and bring to him. A regular express is continually running between Salt Lake City and Oregon Territory.

The San Diego *Herald* gives currency to a report that the Mormons had actually commenced moving towards northern Mexico.

What you can find at Ancestry.com

The article "Religious Records: A Closer Look" featured in *Ancestry* Magazine discusses Latter-day Saint records that are available, including records kept during the time of the Utah War. You can read the article at <www.ancestry.com/learn/library/article.aspx?article=4119>.

You can also find articles about the Utah War by visiting the **Stories & Publications** tab of the **Search** tab at <www.ancestry.com/search/>, then entering "Utah War." You can especially find information in the Historical Newspaper Collection. The excerpt on the previous page is from the *New York Times*, 16 March 1858.

American Civil War, Northern States versus Southern States, 1861–65

THE AMERICAN CIVIL WAR IS A UNIQUE WAR in American history because it was the only war fought between Americans on American soil, rather than against outside forces. This war is among the best known to Americans. The war was fought between industrial-minded Northern states and slavery-based and agricultural Southern states. The two opposing groups had grown further apart because of their differing economic and political interests. One main issue was that the North wanted to abolish slavery, while the South did not, though other issues, such as states' rights, were also involved.

The North leaned toward politics, industry, banking, and manufacturing, while the South focused on agriculture and plantation life, which depended greatly on slaves.

The election of Abraham Lincoln in 1860 was the catalyst for war. With President Lincoln advocating commercial development and containing slavery, the Southern states felt increasingly alienated from the North and were concerned about their future. South Carolina responded to the election by seceding before Lincoln was even inaugurated and also by seizing federal forts in Charleston's harbor. Soon, eleven Southern states had seceded and declared themselves the Confederate States of America, with Jefferson

1857 - 1865

Davis as president. The eleven states that seceded were Alabama, Florida, Georgia, Louisiana, Mississippi, and South Carolina, joined later by Arkansas, North Carolina, Tennessee, Texas, and part of Virginia. The northwest part of Virginia joined the Northern states.

The war became a fight over slavery in the United States, as well as the desire in the North to restore the Union as one United States.

The North had a clear advantage in the war. They had twenty-three states in their favor, including several

border states that favored slavery, as opposed to the eleven Confederate states. The difference was 22 million people to 9 million, of which 3.5 million were slaves. In addition, the North was wealthier and had access to more war supplies, as well as control of the sea and ports. By installing a naval blockade, the North hurt Southern supplies on everything, including food. However, the South had their own advantages. They had more veteran fighters and were more skilled with weapons, and were fighting on their own turf.

The war was separated into three land segments: the East, the West, and the Trans-Mississippi region. In the war in the East, fighting surrounded the two capitals, Washington D.C., and Richmond, Virginia. The Union armies in this area continually failed to defeat the Confederate army, led by General Thomas "Stonewall" Jackson. When General Robert E. Lee was put in command of the Confederate armies in 1862, he led them to victories at Fredericksburg and Chancellorsville. Lee then invaded Pennsylvania in 1863. On the third day of the Battle of Gettysburg, on 3 July 1863, the Union army was able to defend a Confederate infantry assault, but the Confederate troops safely withdrew to Virginia.

In the western theater, Ulysses S. Grant successfully defeated the Confederate armies and took many Confederate fortifications. In the Trans-Mississippi theater, the Union was able to defend against the Confederate's attempts to take Missouri, finally defeating Confederate forces at the Battle of Glorietta Pass on 28 March 1862. The Union defeated the Confederates when Grant and Sherman's troops overcame Lee and Johnston's troops in the East, using their advantages in manpower, industry, and finances. Lee surrendered on 9 April 1865 at Appomattox Courthouse, Virginia, to generous terms that allowed the men to take their horses and go home.

President Lincoln ended the war by urging Americans to reconcile during the reconstruction of the country. On 10 May 1865, new president Andrew Johnson granted amnesty to all Southerners. By then, approximately 970,000 people had died.

What records were generated because of the conflict

During and after the American Civil War, records were kept that provide historians with a great deal of information about where individuals served, their status in the war, who died, who was buried where, and more. These records include enlistment details, national cemeteries where soldiers were buried, lists of regiments, lists of heads of brigades, compiled military service records, pension cards of Civil War veterans, state rosters, regimental histories, photographs, journals, lists of field officers, and lists of prisoners of war.

1861 - 1865

Civil War Soldiers and Sailor System

www.itd.nps.gov/cwss/

A system for finding records of Civil War soldiers and sailors.

The National Archives holds a great deal of these records regarding the Civil War. Visit their website to see what exactly they have available. The Web page called Research in Military Records: Civil War, at <www.archives.gov/research/civil-war/index.html>, contains recommendations on specific microfilm available for the Civil War.

When at the National Archives, head for Room 400.

The National Archives
700 Pennsylvania Avenue NW
Washington, D.C. 20408-0001

Among the useful microfilm at the National Archives are the following:

- *Alphabetical Card Name Index to the Compiled Service Records of Volunteer Soldiers Who Served in Union Organizations Not Raised by the States or Territories, Excepting the Veterans Reserve Corps and the U.S. Colored Troops (M1290).*

- *Compiled Service Records of Former Confederate Soldiers Who Served in the First Through the Sixth U.S. Volunteer Infantry Regiments, 1864–1866 (M1017).*

Also, at the National Archives Military Reference Branch, look for the following:

- RG 109—War Department Collection of Confederate Records

- RG 110—Provost Marshal General's Bureau (Civil War)

A work in progress, the US GenWeb Archives is progressing on the US GenWeb Archives Pension Project to collect and share actual transcriptions from pension records and related pension materials that were developed because of the war. You can view names that are already listed by state, as well as contact a volunteer to become involved in the project at <www.rootsweb.com/%7Eusgenweb/pensions/civilwar/index.htm>.

What you can find at Ancestry.com

Ancestry.com has abundant records from the Civil War that will save many researchers a physical trip to an archive. To view a list of these records, go to the **Search** tab at <www.ancestry.com/search/>. Click "Military Records" in the "Browse Records" section, then click "Civil War Collection." You can also search for "Civil War" on the **Photos & Maps** tab, which will produce thousands of photographs and maps relating to the Civil War. Some of these resources follow:

Andersonville/Civil War Links and Resources

www.ancestry.com/learn/library/article.aspx?article=2393

Andersonville Prisoners of War

www.ancestry.com/search/db.aspx?dbid=3708

Civil War Pension Index: General Index to Pension Files, 1861–1934

www.ancestry.com/search/db.aspx?dbid=4654

Civil War Records: Valuable Sources for Genealogists

www.ancestry.com/learn/library/article. aspx?article=3239

Civil War Research Database

www.ancestry.com/search/rectype/military/cwrd/ main.aspx

Civil War Service Records

www.ancestry.com/search/db.aspx?dbid=4284

Confederate States Field Officers

www.ancestry.com/search/db.aspx?dbid=4537

U.S. Colored Troops Military Service Records, 1861–1865

http://content.ancestry.com/ iexec/?htx=List&dbid=1107

U.S. Civil War Photos, 1860–1870

www.ancestry.com/search/db.aspx?dbid=8759

Spanish-American War, Cuba, Philippine Islands, 1898

CUBA FIRST SOUGHT INDEPENDENCE FROM SPAIN in 1868–78, then gave up for a while. Then, in 1895, they revolted for a second time, seeking assistance from the United States. President Grover Cleveland initially proclaimed neutrality on 12 June 1895 but in December 1896 said that the United States might become involved if Spain proved unable to resolve the Cuba crisis.

The USS Battleship *Maine* in Havana Harbor sank on 15 February 1898. The cause of the explosion was never discovered, but it put Spain in a bad light. Most Americans blamed Spain for not being more responsible for the harbor, thus causing the deaths of the 260 men that died from the ship's explosion. Newspaper giants William Randolph Hearst and Joseph Pulitzer capitalized on the incident, attempting to make Spain look worse because war was good for selling papers. The cry was to "Remember the Maine! To hell with Spain!"

Pressured by newspapers and its influence on the public, the United States declared war on Spain on 20 April 1898, calling it a war defending Cuba's right to independence. On 22 April 1898, the United States

formed a volunteer army that is now known as the Rough Riders, for which Theodore Roosevelt was a lieutenant colonel.

At sea, the U.S. Navy successfully sought out and defeated Spanish ships, killing more than three hundred Spanish near Manila Bay in just one of its successful sea attacks. On land, the Rough Riders suffered found success at the Battle of San Juan Hill but suffered a loss of over fifteen hundred Americans. Several more battles ensued until Spain surrendered at sea, and Santiago surrendered on land.

The Treaty of Paris was signed on 10 December 1898, five months after the initial surrender. In the treaty, the United States was given control over Spain's overseas lands, including Puerto Rico, the Philippines, and Guam. The United States was also given control over the process of Cuba's independence, which was attained in 1902.

What records were generated because of the conflict

The Adjutant General kept records of volunteers for each state. Records were also kept concerning pensions and naval officers.

At the National Archives, records of interest include the following:

- *General Index to Compiled Service Records of Volunteer Soldiers Who Served During the War with Spain* (M871)

- *Register of Enlistments in the U.S. Army, 1798–1914* (M233)

- *General Index to Pension Files, 1861–1934* (T288)

- *Abstracts of Service Records of Naval Officers ("Records of Officers"), 1829–1924* (M1328)

- *General and Special Indexes to the General Correspondence of the Office of the Secretary of the Navy, July 1897–Aug. 1926* (M1052)

- *Letters Received by the Commission Branch of the Adjutant General's Office, 1863–1870, 527 rolls* (M1064)

- *Name and Subject Index to the Letters Received by the Appointment, Commission, and Personal Branch of the Adjutant General's Office, 1871–1894, 4 rolls.* (M1125)

- *Index to the General Correspondence of the Office of the Adjutant General, 1890–1917, 1,269 rolls* (M698)

- *Documents Relating to the Military and Naval Service of Blacks Awarded the Congressional Medal of Honor from the Civil War to the Spanish American War, 4 rolls* (M929)

At the Library of Congress, look for *Manuscript Division—Reference Index for the Dictionary Catalog of Collections* in the Spanish-American war section.

1898

The US GenWeb Archives is progressing on the US GenWeb Archives Pension Project to collect and share transcriptions from pension records and related pension materials developed because of the war. You can view names already listed by state, as well as contact a volunteer to become involved in the project at <www.rootsweb.com/%7Eusgenweb/pensions/spnamer/index.htm>.

You can also visit <www.accessgenealogy.com/military/spanish/index.htm> and scroll toward the second half of the page to view a list of states with links to their rosters.

What you can find at Ancestry.com

You will find the following at Ancestry.com:

Massachusetts Spanish American War Records

www.ancestry.com/search/db.aspx?dbid=5070

Find details about the 8th Massachusetts Infantry Roll of Honor as collected by Debra F. Graden from *Twelve Months with the Eighth Massachusetts Infantry in the Service of the United States,* located at the C.A.R.L. Library at Ft. Leavenworth, Kansas.

North Carolina Volunteers, Spanish American War

www.ancestry.com/search/db.aspx?dbid=4136

Spanish-American Family History Guide

www.ancestry.com/search/db.aspx?dbid=4126

This guide contains many family pedigrees of Spanish-American families, as well as an address listing of some of the most helpful repositories of Spanish, Mexican, and Spanish-American records.

Connecticut Servicemen, Spanish American War

www.ancestry.com/search/db.aspx?dbid=3803

This record was taken from the Records of Service of Connecticut Men in the Army, Navy, and Marine Corps of the United States in the Spanish-American War, and includes the names of thirty-eight hundred men from Connecticut.

Indiana Spanish American War Records

www.ancestry.com/search/db.aspx?dbid=4305

This record includes the names of over seventy-eight hundred Indiana men who volunteered in the war.

Minnesota Volunteers in the Spanish American War and the Philippine Insurrection

www.ancestry.com/search/db.aspx?dbid=4816

Ohio Solders in the War with Spain, 1898–99

www.ancestry.com/search/db.aspx?dbid=5306

Oregon Volunteers, Spanish American War and the Philippine Insurrection

www.ancestry.com/search/db.aspx?dbid=4830

Spanish American War Resources from the *Ancestry Daily News*

www.ancestry.com/learn/library/article.aspx?article=3775

Goff's Historical Map of the United States

http://search.ancestry.com/cgi-bin/sse.dll?indiv=1&db=LOCMaps%2c&rank=1&f3=Goff%27s+historical+map+of+the+United+States&f7=&f10=&year=&yearend=&gskw=&ti=0&ti.si=0&gss=angs-d&fh=0&recid=348&recoff=121+122+123+124+125+126+127+134+137

This military map of the mid-Atlantic states outlines the paths taken in the Civil War, Spanish American War, and the Philippine Insurrection.

Philippine Insurrection, Philippine Islands, 1899–1902

AFTER THE SPANISH AMERICAN WAR, Emilio Aguinaldo, a Philippine independence fighter, expected the United States to give the Philippines their independence. When the United States refused, war broke out, with a Filipino army of seventy thousand. The Filipinos resisted the American army until 1902, introducing guerrilla warfare into their fighting. When the war ended, Congress passed the Philippine Government Act, which allowed the Philippines a great deal of self government, though they were not independent from the United States. By then, five thousand Americans had died. In addition, the Americans had forced many civilians into concentration camps, where thousands died.

What records were generated because of the conflict

The National Archives houses compiled service records of the volunteer soldiers in the Philippine Insurrection.

At the National Archives, look for the following:

- *Index to Compiled Service Records of Volunteer Soldiers Who Served During the Philippine Insurrection* (M872). This record details the soldier's name, rank, and unit.

You can also search online for the names of the soldiers who served during the Philippine Insurrection at the Kansas State Historical Society website: <www.kshs.org/genealogists/military/adjgenlspanam.htm>.

What you can find at Ancestry.com

From the **Search** tab at Ancestry.com <www.ancestry.com/search/>, click the **Photos & Maps** tab. Enter "Philippine Insurrection" in the "Keywords" field. There are two images from the Library of Congress Photo Collection, 1840–2000 regarding this war, one of which is shown here:

World War I, Europe, 1914–18

WORLD WAR I WAS TRIGGERED when the heir to the Austria-Hungarian throne, Archduke Franz Ferdinand, was assassinated by a Serbian nationalist on 28 June 1914. In response, Austria demanded punishment of Serbia. Austria backed its demand with support from their ally, Germany. However, Serbia also had allies—Russia, whose own allies were France and Britain. These occurred in the years leading up to the assassination when countries in Europe started forming alliances with each other, often in secret. The domino effect of the many alliances and the outcry from the assassination lead to nearly thirty countries being involved with the war, including countries that were not tied to alliances.

The war was divided into two opposing groups known as the Allies and the Central Powers. The Allies were led by Russia, Britain, and France, later joined by the United States and Italy. Australia, Canada, and New Zealand were among other countries that also sided with the Allies. The Central Powers were led by Germany, Austria-Hungary, and Turkey and also included Bulgaria and the Ottoman Empire.

The leaders of the initial countries involved generally believed a war between them would end by Christmas, but instead it lasted four years.

The United States became involved on 6 April 1917 after Germany attempted to bribe Mexico with the territory it had lost in 1848 if it would declare war on

America. In addition, on 7 May 1915, Germany sank the British passenger liner *Lusitania* with a U-boat, killing 128 Americans. Germany alienated America when it refused to comply with President Wilson's demands to restrict submarine warfare.

When America joined the war by declaring its intent against Germany, the Allies had the edge they needed over the Central Powers. On 11 November 1918, Germany signed an armistice. Afterward, the Treaty of Versailles was signed and the League of Nations was developed. Though both the treaty and the league came about because of President Wilson's efforts, the other countries wanted to punish Germany severely, despite President Wilson's wishes for a simple peace proposal, which included what he called his Fourteen Points.

As a result, the United States Senate would not ratify the treaty, which placed full blame for the war on Germany and demanded Germany pay a huge sum for the war to certain countries. The German economy was severely damaged, resulting in famine and great bitterness toward other countries. Ironically, President Wilson had wanted a treaty that would seek world peace because he feared that too harsh a punishment would lead to future wars. His fears came true in World War II, when Adolf Hitler would take control of much of Western Europe using what he considered to be the unfair treatment at the end of World War I as his motive.

When World War I ended, over 9 million people were dead, including more than 115,000 Americans. The war had been complex in many ways. Many events occurred that built distrust and competition between the countries. The unification of Germany and the unification of Italy added two great powers in Europe, making other countries uneasy and leading to both public and secret treaties between countries. In addition there was already a growing sense of rivalry as the European nations began seeking new terrains for their rapidly expanding economies. Another factor was a massive arms race. The war introduced a variety of new weapons, such as machine guns, boats, U-boats, and poison gas.

The war reshaped our ancestors' lives geographically by moving country boundaries and bringing people under the rule of different countries. For instance, Hungary became one-third of its prewar size. In addition, nearly three million Austro-Germans suddenly became part of Czechoslovakia.

What records were generated because of the conflict

When the U.S. Congress officially declared war against Germany on 6 April 1917, it began a Selective Service Act to draft American men. The government issued registration cards for three separate birth-date ranges and issued them in June 1917, June and August 1918, and September 1918. Depending on the date range, registrants were asked to answer twelve, ten, or twenty

1899 - 1918

57

questions, ranging from name and address to physical description to name of employer and nearest relative. In addition, the United States kept records of soldiers who died in the war. For instance, the American Battle Monuments Commission is responsible for twenty-four American cemeteries that are located in foreign countries.

At the National Archives, look for the following:

- *Index to Rendezvous Reports, Armed Guard Personnel, 1917–1920* (T1101)

- *Index to Rendezvous Reports, Naval Auxiliary Service, 1917–1919* (T1100)

- *Records of the 27th Division of the American Expeditionary Forces, 1917–1919* (M819)

Also, visit the National Archives online at <www. archives.gov/research/military/ww1.html>. This website contains a list of links to records in the National Archives.

At the Military Reference Branch of the National Archives, look for the following:

- RG 77—Office of the Chief of Engineers. It includes records like a card catalog showing origin, authorization, and mobilization of engineer units, World War I, 1914.

- RG 120—American Expeditionary Forces (World War I), 1917–18. It includes records from war diaries to casualty lists and prisoner of war records.

At the Library of Congress, look for the following:

- *Manuscript Division—Reference Index for the Dictionary Catalog of Collections.*

As one of the most remembered wars in our nation's history, and a relatively recent war, World War I records are widely documented throughout the nation. Each state is likely to house some records about soldiers who fought in World War I.

Visit Online World War I Indexes & Records at <www. militaryindexes.com/worldwarone/> for a list of links to various databases about World War I offered by various states.

What you can find at Ancestry.com

Ancestry.com offers a wide variety of World War I records, including draft records, which typically include the birth date, birth location, father's birthplace, and the address of the next of kin for 24 million men born between 1873 and 1900.

The following records could prove useful:

World War I Draft Registration Cards, 1917–1918

http://content.ancestry.com/iexec/?htx=List&dbid=6482

An example of a World War I draft card is shown below. To help you decipher World War I draft registration cards, download PDF versions of the blank draft registration cards for free at <www.ancestry.com/save/charts/WWI.htm>.

U.S. World War I Mothers' Pilgrimage, 1930

www.ancestry.com/search/db.aspx?dbid=4224

After World War I, the War Department of the United States compiled a list of mothers and widows of soldiers killed in World War I, giving them the opportunity to visit their deceased son's or husband's final resting place in Europe. This database lists 11,000 women who qualified for the trip, according to department records on 15 November 1929, and includes name, city and state of residence, and relationship to the deceased, as well as the soldier's name, rank, unit, and cemetery.

WWI Civilian Draft Registrations

www.ancestry.com/search/db.aspx?dbid=3172

The World War I Civilian Draft Registration generally includes the name, birth date, father's birthplace, and address of next of kin, among other information, for 1.2 million United States men. The men registered were born between 1873 and 1900 and completed their draft registration cards in 1917 and 1918. An example of a World War I Civilian Draft Registration card is shown on the previous page.

American Soldiers of World War I

http://content.ancestry.com/
iexec/?htx=List&dbid=7399

This record of American soldiers who died in World War I is arranged alphabetically by state. Details include photographs, name, rank, and cause of death—ranging from disease to battle wounds. This record is compiled from Haulsee, W.M., comp. *Soldiers of the Great War. Vol. I–III.* Washington, D.C.: Soldiers Record, 1920.

WWI, WWII, and Korean War Casualty Listings

www.ancestry.com/search/db.aspx?dbid=8853

U.S. Naval Deaths, World War I

www.ancestry.com/search/db.aspx?dbid=4022

You can also search the historical photo collection at Ancestry.com to view photographs taken from World War I. The accompanying image (on the previous page) is a postcard from this collection.

World War II, Europe, Asia, the Pacific, Africa, 1939–45

THE FIGHT FOR POWER AND TERRITORY IN EUROPE and Asia primarily by Germany and Japan, led to the full-scale war that eventually involved over seventy nations and resulted in the deaths of between 40 and 50 million people, including an estimated 6 million who died in the Holocaust.

Historians trace causes of the war back twenty years to the end of World War I, when, in the wake of the war, boundary lines were changed and Germany in particular lost a great deal of territory, which Hitler openly sought to regain. In the years leading up to World War II, many other countries were also actively trying to establish their power in Europe. For instance, Italy invaded Ethiopia in 1935 and Albania in 1939.

By 1940, Hitler had successfully taken over most of western Europe. Germany continued to invade European countries, taking Paris by 5 June 1940 and invading Russia on 22 June 1941. Japan began rapidly expanding their territory soon after Hitler, initially resigning from the League of Nations in 1941 when they were asked to remove themselves from Manchuria, which they had invaded. They continued to conquer neighboring areas, taking Peking, China, in 1937 and had French Indochina, Wake Island, Hong Kong, and the Philippines by 1942.

America tried to maintain an isolationism stance

throughout these European wars, but when the Japanese invaded French Indochina in 25 July 1941, America refused all trading with Japan. Many historians look at this moment as a turning point that led Japan to attack America.

World War II officially began on 3 September 1939, when Great Britain and France declared war on Germany after it refused to withdraw from Poland, which it had invaded two days before. That same day, a German submarine torpedoed a British ship, killing twenty-eight Americans. While the United States continued to maintain a policy of not becoming involved, they did send arms and select supplies to France and Britain.

In 1941, German U-boats torpedoed two ships, killing eleven Americans in one ship and one hundred Americans in the second ship, bringing America closer to war with Germany. Then, the trigger point happened for the United States. On 7 December 1941, Japan attacked the United States naval base at Pearl Harbor in Hawaii, killing 2,403 people. The United States declared war on Japan the next day.

On 11 December 1941, Japan, Germany, and Italy declared war on the United States. The world was then officially divided into two groups known as the Allied Powers, which included the United States, the Soviet Union, and the United Kingdom, and the Axis Powers, which included Germany, Italy, and Japan.

The war consisted of numerous invasions throughout Europe and deadly battles but reached a turning point on D-Day, 6 June 1944. On that day, the Allied Powers lead the largest invasion in history, with over 175,000 troops. Though many soldiers died, the Germans were driven back by the invasion. This event marked the turning point in the defeat of the Axis Powers. Then, in December 1944, at the Battle of the Bulge, Hitler failed in his last major attempt to push the Allies back. On 30 April 1945, Hitler committed suicide. The German forces were spread through various countries but surrendered in May 1945.

The Japanese were contained separately, with American soldiers and marines moving from island to island in the Pacific, seeking out the Japanese soldiers. The fighting was significantly worse in Okinawa, south of Japan. Finally, President Harry Truman reluctantly ordered the dropping of the two atomic bombs that President Roosevelt had set in motion. The first bomb was dropped on Hiroshima on 6 August 1945, and the next on Nagasaki on 9 August 1945. The first bomb alone killed or seriously injured 180,000 Japanese. The Japanese surrendered on 14 August 1945.

What records were generated because of the conflict

During World War II, over 100,000 Japanese-Americans from Washington, Oregon, and California were sent to internment camps in Arkansas, California, Colorado, Idaho, Utah, and Wyoming. Records were kept of these moves, including everything from name and previous address to highest level of education and pension information.

Records for World War II also include enlistment and registration records, casualty records, and more.

At the National Archives, look for the following:

- *Mission and Combat Reports of the Fifth Fighter Command, 1942–1945* (M1065)

- *Missing Air Crew Reports of the U.S. Army Air Forces, 1942–1945* (M1380)

Also, visit the National Archives online at <www.archives.gov/research/ww2/>.

This Web page contains a list of links to records that the National Archives holds and some information about those records.

At the Library of Congress, look for the following:

- *Manuscript Division — Reference Index for the Dictionary Catalog of Collections.*

What you can find at Ancestry.com

Ancestry.com offers a wide variety of World War II records, including draft records, which typically include the birth date, birth location, father's birthplace, and the address of the next of kin for 5.9 million men born between 1873 and 1900.

Be sure to take a look at the following databases:

U.S. World War II Draft Registration Cards, 1942

www.ancestry.com/search/db.aspx?dbid=1002

This collection is the "old man's draft," the only World War II draft registration cards currently available to the public. It is called the "old man's draft" because the men required to register were forty-five to sixty-five years old. The image below is an example of these cards.

U.S. World War II Army Enlistment Records, 1938–1946

www.ancestry.com/search/db.aspx?dbid=8939

World War II and Korean Conflict Veterans Interred Overseas

www.ancestry.com/search/db.aspx?dbid=4283

WWI, WWII, and Korean War Casualty Listings

www.ancestry.com/search/db.aspx?dbid=8853

Japanese Americans Relocated During World War II
about Kataro Saimoto

Name:	**Kataro Saimoto**
Project:	Gila River (Pima, Sacaton)
Assembly:	Turlook
Gender:	Male
Race:	Japanese
Birth Year:	1889
Birth Place Region:	Urban Prefectures (Kyoto, Osaka and Tokyo)
Birth Place Country:	Japan
US Arrival Year:	1907
City:	Los Angeles
State:	California
Language:	Japanese Speak, Write, Read; English Speak, Read & Write
School Years Japan:	13 Years
School Years Japan Other:	1-8, 9-12 & 13 Or More Years Of School Only
Education Degree:	No Degree
Grade Completed:	College 3 In U.S.
Total Time In Japan:	15 Years But Less Than 20 In Japan
Times In Japan:	1 Time-- Not Attending School
Age While In Japan:	Between Ages 0-9 & Also 10-19
Service Or Pensions:	X
Marital Status:	Married
Race Spouse:	Japanese
Alien Reg Number:	Has A.R. But Not S.S. Number And Has Not Attended Japanese Language School
Religion:	Not Available
Primary Occupation:	Salesmen, Real Estate
Secondary Occupation:	Retail Managers
Tertiary Occupation:	Nursery Operators and Flower Growers
File Number:	30972771164
Mother Birth Location:	Japan
Father Birth Location:	Japan
Father U.S. Occupation:	Blank, Unknown, None, Dash
Father Occupation Other:	Managerial & Official (Except Farm); Comparable United States Employment Service Code Numbers 0-7 Thru 0-99. See Documentation.
Spouse Race:	Japanese

Save This Record
Attach this record to a person in your tree as a source record, or save for later evaluation.

[Save ⊡]

Japanese Americans Relocated During World War II

www.ancestry.com/search/db.aspx?dbid=8918

Young American Patriots

www.ancestry.com/search/db.aspx?dbid=8941

Generally published in the Southern States, these books were published soon after World War II ended and include photographs and biographical sketches of soldiers for states including West Virginia, North Carolina, Pennsylvania, Kentucky, Virginia, Ohio, Maryland, Delaware, and South Carolina.

WWII *Stars and Stripes* Newspaper

www.ancestry.com/search/db.aspx?dbid=1136

This newspaper was widely read by United States troops, and it provides some historical perspective.

Korean War, Korea, 1950–53

AFTER WORLD WAR II ENDED, KOREA WAS DIVIDED by the United States and the Soviet Union without consulting Korea. The two halves, North Korea and South Korea, sought reunification, but under rules that would favor their own halves of the country. This was the setup to the Korean War, which the United States officially called the Korean Conflict and the Koreans know as either 6-25 or the Fatherland Liberation War. The war began on 25 June 1950, when ninety thousand North Korean troops invaded South Korea.

President Truman came to South Korea's defense, sending U.S. Navy and Air Force, but North Korea captured the capitol, Seoul, within three days. Within a month, the United Nations had met several times, first to pass a resolution adopting a cease-fire, then to commit to support the South Korean government, then to acknowledge American leadership in the UN forces. Under General Douglas MacArthur's leadership, UN

troops were able to recapture Seoul by 15 September 1950.

At this point, the war shifted goals. Originally, South Korea was fighting against the invasion, but once North Korea was pushed back to its original boundary lines, UN forces began invading North Korea with the goal to unite Korea under South Korean President Syngman Rhee's rule, overthrowing the communist government. When the UN forces began taking action against communist North Korea, communist China became involved, first threatening, then attacking South Korea. By 6 November 1950, one million Chinese were in Korea.

General MacArthur sought to fight China, while President Truman sought peace. Much of the United States sided with MacArthur, but President Truman replaced MacArthur with a new general, and on 10 July 1951, the UN and China began peace talks. However, more fighting continued until the end of July, when a treaty was signed permanently separating communist North Korea from democratic South Korea.

What records were generated because of the conflict

The Veterans Administration has kept records of prisoners of war. Some of these details are not available to the public because many of these individuals are still living, so the names are not released to preserve their privacy. The Office of the Secretary of Defense also kept records of deaths caused by hostilities, as well as details on missing or captured soldiers. In addition, the Adjutant General's Office offers some information about casualties.

You can contact the Center for Electronic Records to request copies of data from Department of Defense lists, army lists, and not recovered or missing lists, at the following address:

> National Archives II
> University of Maryland
> 8601 Adelphi Road
> College Park, Maryland 10740-6001
> (410) 713-6800

Also, consider visiting the National Archives online at <www.archives.gov/research/ww2/>, which contains a list of links to records the National Archives holds, including the following:

- RG 319—Records of the Army Staff. This includes details of American prisoners of war during the Korean War.

- RG 407—Records of the Adjutant General's Office. This includes details of Korean War dead and wounded.

The National Archives also provides a list of Korean War casualties based on the individual's home state, and extracted from the military casualty data files in the

Records of the Office of the Secretary of Defense (RG 330) at following Web address <www.archives.gov/research/korean-war/casualty-lists/state-level-alpha.html>.

The Department of Defense established an official website to commemorate the 50th anniversary of the Korean War on 25 June 2000. The website displays photographs and historical information about the war, including Medal of Honor recipients. You can view the name, rank, citation details, and more for individuals that received a Medal of Honor for service during the Korean War at <http://korea50.army.mil/history/moh.shtml>.

The RootsWeb.com POW-MIA Records is a free database that you can search at <http://userdb.rootsweb.com/pow_mia/> for soldiers that were either missing or prisoners of war during either the Korean War or the Vietnam War. Most of the information for this database comes from the United States Department of Defense, Defense Prisoner of War/Missing Personnel Office at <www.dtic.mil/dpmo/>.

What you can find at Ancestry.com
You can find the following resources on Ancestry.com:

World War II and Korean Conflict Veterans Interred Overseas

www.ancestry.com/search/db.aspx?dbid=4283

Korean War Prisoners of War, 1950–1954

www.ancestry.com/search/db.aspx?dbid=8850

Korean War Casualties, 1950–1957

www.ancestry.com/search/db.aspx?dbid=1033

WWI, WWII, and Korean War Casualty Listings

www.ancestry.com/search/db.aspx?dbid=8853

Vietnam War, Vietnam, 1954–75

THE VIETNAM WAR IS KNOWN to the Vietnamese as the American War, or more specifically, the "War Against the Americans and to Save the Nation." The war took place between 1954 and 1975 and was fought between the coalition forces, which consisted of the United States, the Republic of Vietnam, Australia, New Zealand, and South Korea, and the opposing forces, which consisted of North Vietnam and the National Liberation Front, which was a communist-led South Vietnamese guerrilla movement. Though the USSR chose to stay out of the battle, they provided the latter group with military aid.

In northern Vietnam, Ho Chi Minh was seeking elections that would place him and his communist

regime in power. In southern Vietnam, Ngo Dinh Diem was refusing the elections because he knew the communists would win the vote over the noncommunists. The United States stepped in to help prevent the elections, sending 16,600 military advisors to Vietnam.

President Lyndon B. Johnson found the excuse he needed to send combat troops into Vietnam when on August 1964, some North Vietnamese allegedly assaulted American naval vessels in the Tonkin Gulf of Vietnam. However, Americans were growing anti-war by 1968, especially after it was revealed to the public that 347 Vietnamese civilians were massacred at the small Vietnamese village of My Lai. The Charlie Company had arrived at the village expecting to find signs of a stronghold with weapons but upon being wrong, shot all villagers anyway, including women and children, and destroyed the village.

When Richard Nixon took Johnson's place as the new president, he began a process of training and equipping the Southern Vietnamese to defend their country, finally removing all forces on 29 April 1975. The North Vietnamese successfully invaded South Vietnam the next day. In the wake of the unification of North and South Vietnam, hundreds of supporters of the South Vietnamese government were executed.

What records were generated because of the conflict

During the Vietnam War, the Secretary of Defense collected 58,152 names of casualties, including casualties from Cambodia, Communist China, Laos, North Vietnam, South Vietnam, and Thailand. The National Archives also kept records of awards and honors given to U.S. and allied foreign military personnel during the Vietnam War between 1965–1972.

The Center for Electronic Records can provide copies of data from Department of Defense lists and army lists at the following address:

> National Archives II
> University of Maryland
> 8601 Adelphi Road
> College Park, Maryland 10740-6001
> (410) 713-6800

The National Archives also provides a list of Vietnam War casualties based on the individual's home state, extracted from the military casualty data files in the Records of the Office of the Secretary of Defense (RG 330) at <www.archives.gov/research/vietnam-war/casualty-lists/state-level-alpha.html>.

Also, consider visiting the National Archives online list of Vietnam War–related electronic records at <www.archives.gov/research/vietnam-war/electronic-records.html>.

The RootsWeb.com POW-MIA Records is a free database that you can search at <http://userdb. rootsweb.com/pow_mia/> for soldiers that were either missing or prisoners of war during either the Korean War or the Vietnam War. Most of the information here comes from the United States Department of Defense, Defense Prisoner of War/Missing Personnel Office at <www.dtic.mil/dpmo/>.

What you can find at Ancestry.com

You will find the following records at Ancestry.com:

Vietnam War, Awards and Decorations of Honor, 1965–1972

www.ancestry.com/search/db.aspx?dbid=8847

Vietnam War, Casualties Returned Alive, 1962–1979

www.ancestry.com/search/db.aspx?dbid=8846

Vietnam War, U.S. Military Casualties, 1956–1998

www.ancestry.com/search/db.aspx?dbid=3095

U.S. Army Personnel and Dependent Casualties, 1961–1981

www.ancestry.com/search/db.aspx?dbid=8849

1954 – 1975

★　　★　　★

ADDITIONAL RESOURCES AND BIBLIOGRAPHY

Additional Resources

THIS BOOK WAS DESIGNED TO HELP researchers get a quick jump-start on researching the military records of their ancestors.

When you're ready to go more in-depth, or to supplement your research, check out these resources:

U.S. Military Records, A Guide to Federal & State Sources
by James C. Neagles.
This book from Ancestry Publishing is a hefty 400+ pages and discusses military records from the perspective of types of records made, resources at the various National Archives and history and research centers, state resources, and published sources. The Local History and Genealogy Reference Specialist for the Library of Congress, Judith P. Reid, said this book was "destined to become a classic…a standout in the field."

The Source, A Guidebook to American Genealogy, Third Edition,
edited by Loretto Dennis Szucs and Sandra Hargreaves Luebking
This comprehensive guide is considered by many genealogists to be a must-have. It is intended to be the primary resource for both beginning and advanced researchers. Many of the individual chapters are authored by leaders in the genealogy community, often regarding their specialty.

Access to Archival Databases (AAD)
http://aad.archives.gov/aad/
The National Archives has an online Archival Database that can be both searched and browsed. Categories include browsing by wars, places, time spans, and more.

The Library of Congress

The Library of Congress holds an extensive collection of publications that covers the wars in which the United States was involved. You can find military references in both the Local History and Genealogy Reading Room and the Main Reading Room. Check the Manuscript Division Reading Room for over 10,000 collections of personal papers.

Daughters of the American Revolution

The National Society Daughters of the American Revolution has 125,000 publications by subject or state. You can visit them at the following address:

> 1776 D Street NW
> Washington, D.C. 20006-5392
> (202) 879-3229

Medal of Honor Recipients

www.army.mil/cmh-pg/moh1.htm

The U.S. Army Center of Military History lists all of their Medal of Honor recipients online, arranged alphabetically with the war for which they received their honor. Details include name, rank, organization, citation, and more. The website also provides Medal of Honor statistics, among other facts.

Databases at Ancestry.com

With over four billion names in their database, Ancestry.com has countless other records not listed in this book. Try searching by State to find other military records specifically made in the state which your ancestor was from. Also, see these other databases not previously listed in this book:

U.S. Veterans Gravesites, ca.1775–2006

www.ancestry.com/search/db.aspx?dbid=8750

This database covers cemeteries nationwide that hold the remains of U.S. veterans and their dependants, with information ranging from interment date to veteran service dates.

U.S. Military Records, 1925: Official National Guard Register

www.ancestry.com/search/db.aspx?dbid=4996

This database includes the name, rank, regiment, company, birth date, birthplace, and state of officers and sergeant instructors from 1925.

U.S. Army Historical Register, 1789–1903, Vol. 1

www.ancestry.com/search/db.aspx?dbid=3122

This database is an alphabetical list of over 17,500 officers who served in the United States Army from 1789–1903. Data includes name, rank attained, and state where appointed.

U.S. Army Historical Register, 1789–1903, Vol. 2

www.ancestry.com/search/db.aspx?dbid=3167

This database is an alphabetical list of over 48,000 officers who served in the United States Army from 1789–1903. Data includes name, rank attained, and state where appointed.

Naval Pensioners of the United States

http://content.ancestry.com/
iexec/?htx=BookList&dbid=
49267

This database shows the pension records of approximately three thousand seamen and sailors who were awarded pensions as a result of various acts between 1800 and 1851.

National Home for Disabled Volunteer Soldiers

www.ancestry.com/search/db.aspx?dbid=6258

This database was complied from a report from the National Home for Disabled Volunteer Soldiers for the fiscal year ending 30 June 1895. Details include name of soldier, company or regiment, length of service, occupation, and more.

Marine Corps Muster Rolls 1893–1940

www.ancestry.com/search/db.aspx?dbid=1089

This database includes periodic lists of the marines serving on each ship in the navy or wherever else they were stationed. The Marine Corps Muster Rolls are also available at the National Archives.

Bibliography

Reference Books

Davis, Kenneth C. *Don't Know Much About History*. New York, NY: Harper Collins Publishers Inc., 2003.

Neagles, James C. *U.S. Military Records, A Guide to Federal & State Sources*. Orem, Utah: Ancestry Publishing, 1994.

Neville, John D. comp. *Bacon's Rebellion: Abstracts of Materials in the Colonial Records Project*. Jamestown: Jamestown Foundation, 1976.

Potter, Chandler E. *The Military History of the State of New Hampshire, 1623–1861, From Its Settlement, in 1623, to the Rebellion, in 1861…Biographical Notices of Many of the Officers…*Concord: 1866 [1868]. Reprint "with added indexes…." Baltimore: Genealogical Publishing Co., 1972.

Richards, Henry M.M. *The Pennsylvania-German in the French and Indian War: A Historical Sketch…Pennsylvania German Society Proceedings and Addresses of 1905*. Vol. 15. Lancaster: PGS, 1905.

Szucs, Loretto Dennis, and Sandra Hargreaves Luebking. *The Source: A Guidebook to American Genealogy*. Third ed. Provo, Utah: Ancestry Publishing, 2006.

Taylor, Philip F. *A Calendar of the Warrants for Land in*

Kentucky, Granted for Service in the French and Indian War. Baltimore: Genealogical Publishing Co., 1967.

Whipkey, Harry E. *Guide to the Manuscript Groups in the Pennsylvania State Archives.* Harrisburg: Pennsylvania Historical and Museum Commission, 1976.

References Online

American History Timelines, American Involvement in Wars from Colonial Times to the Present
http://americanhistory.about.com/library/timelines/bltimelineuswars.htm

America's Wars: U.S. Casualties and Veterans
www.infoplease.com/ipa/A0004615.html

Ancestry Daily News
www.ancestry.com/learn/library/article.aspx?article=2115

Access Genealogy
www.accessgenealogy.com/military/spanish/index.htm

The Legacy of King Philip's War: 1998
www.georgetown.edu/users/arsenauj/kpw.html

U.S. District Court for the Phoenix Division of the District of Arizona
http://germanroots.home.att.net/arizona.html

Online World War I Indexes & Records
www.militaryindexes.com/worldwarone/

Soldiers in King Philip's War
http://books.google.com/books?id=BtGm3zlgd NoC&dq=Mr.+John+Hull+Massachusetts+Colony +&pg=RA2-PA1&ots=DOr-nfgO1N&sig=xUc7g3_ p5YGXK6f4kKeVjoKJvdg&prev=www.google.com/ search%3Fhl%3Den%26q%3DMr.%2BJohn%2BHull% 2BMassachusetts%2BColony%2B%26btnG%3DSearch &sa=X&oi=print&ct=result&cd=1#PPP14,M1

Genealogical Records of the War of 1812
www.archives.gov/publications/prologue/1991/ winter/war-of-1812.html
www.archives.gov/research/arc/topics/revolutionary-war. html#pension

The Pequot War
www.amazon.com/exec/obidos/ASIN/1558490302/ ref=nosim/collegiateway

The History of Philip's War: Commonly Called the Great

Indian War of 1675 and 1676, revised edition
www.1st-hand-history.org/Church/album1.html

Encyclopedia Britannica Online
www.britannica.com/eb/article-247841/Jamestown-Colony

Native Americans and American History
www.cr.nps.gov/history/resedu/native_americans.pdf

The Great War and the Shaping of the 20th Century
www.pbs.org/greatwar/

Grolier Online
www.grolier.com/wwii/wwii_1.html

The Guardroom, Games & Fun Limited Trading, 2002
www.guardroom.co.uk/chrono.htm

HighBeam Encyclopedia
www.encyclopedia.com/doc/1O48-ShayssRebellion.html
www.encyclopedia.com/doc/1E1-VietnamW.html
www.encyclopedia.com/doc/1E1-WW1.html

History of Jamestown
www.apva.org/history/index.html

Kansas State Historical Society
www.kshs.org/genealogists/military/adjgenlspanam.htm

42Explore
www.42explore2.com/ww1.htm

Massachusetts Archives Collection Database (1629–1799)
www.sec.state.ma.us/ArchivesSearch/RevolutionarySearch.aspx

The National Archive: eVetRecs
www.archives.gov/veterans/evetrecs/

National Park Service
www.nps.gov/archive/colo/Jthanout/BacRebel.html

National WWII Memorial, Washington, D.C.
www.wwiimemorial.com/default.asp?page=facts.asp&subpage=intro
www.cyberdriveillinois.com/departments/archives/di/955__002.htm

The New Jersey Historical Society
www.jerseyhistory.org/arch_military.html

Ohio History Central—Pontiac's Rebellion
www.ohiohistorycentral.org/entry.php?rec=539

Pennsylvania State Archives

www.phmc.state.pa.us/Bah/DAM/military/fiwar.htm

www.digitalarchives.state.pa.us/archive.asp

Remember, Understand Honor and Give from the Heart

www.pearlharbormemorial.com/site/pp.asp?c=fqLQJ2NNG&b=386117&msource=gphw06

RJO's Ancestors in American Colonial Wars, 1637–1763

http://rjohara.net/gen/wars/

Soldiers in King Philips' War

www.usgennet.org/usa/topic/newengland/philip/1-10/preface.html

Statistical Summary America's Major Wars

www.cwc.lsu.edu/other/stats/warcost.htm

The U.S. Army Heritage & Education Center

www.carlisle.army.mil/ahec/

USA History Wars – King George's War: War of the Austrian Succession

www.usahistory.com/wars/austsucc.htm

The US GenWeb Archives Pension Project

www.rootsweb.com/%7Eusgenweb/pensions/

Vietnam War

www.vietnam-war.info/summary/

Virtual Jamestown, Robert Beverley's Description of the 1622 Indian Attack

www.virtualjamestown.org

Wikipedia

www.wikipedia.com

World War II

www.answers.com/topic/world-war-ii

The World of 1898: The Spanish-American War

www.loc.gov/rr/hispanic/1898/intro.html

Printed in the USA
CPSIA information can be obtained
at www.ICGtesting.com
JSHW070801230124
55856JS00037B/112